D1570978

LOCKE, JEFFERSON
AND THE JUSTICES:

Foundations and Failures
of the US Government

For Michael with highest regard.

George

LOCKE, JEFFERSON and the JUSTICES:

Foundations and Failures of the US Government

by

George M. Stephens

Preface by
Newt Gingrich

Algora Publishing
New York

Algora Publishing, New York
© 2002 by Algora Publishing
All rights reserved. Published 2002.
Printed in the United States of America
ISBN: 1-892941-96-1 (softcover)
ISBN: 1-892941-97-X (hardcover)

Editors@algora.com

  Library of Congress Cataloging-in-Publication Data

Stephens, George M.
  Locke, Jefferson, and the justices : foundations and failures
of the US government / by George M. Stephens.
      p. cm.
  ISBN 1-892941-96-1 (alk. paper)
  1. Constitutional history--United States. 2. Civil rights--
United States. 3. Law and politics. I. Title.
  KF4541 .S693 2002
  342.73'029--dc21
                          2002000899

New York
www.algora.com

To Karin.

TABLE OF CONTENTS

Preface

This book is about John Locke's influence on American politics and law; it is also about the roots of the Contract with America, which seeks to renew the American Dream by promoting individual liberty, economic opportunity, and personal responsibility, through limited and effective government, high standards of performance, and an America strong enough to defend all her citizens against violence at home or abroad.

The Contract stems from the Constitution, the Declaration of Independence and John Locke's writings on government and religion. The Contract is an instrument to help repair a fundamental disconnection between citizens and their elected officials. It has five principles for the basic philosophy of American civilization:

- individual liberty
- economic opportunity
- limited government
- personal responsibility
- security at home and abroad.

In my own speeches and writings, I stress that we have an extraordinarily instructive text by which to guide ourselves — our own history. Becoming aware of our own history and recovering parts of our lost heritage promises a solution to many of our problems.

In this book, George Stephens has traced our political and legal history back to its origins — especially to John Locke, from whom our founders took our systems of rights and responsibilities. It was Locke who placed rights with the individual; who advocated limited government; who said that people should take personal responsibility by working out their contracts; who said that government has legitimacy only as a contract with its people to preserve their rights; and who explained that security of life, liberty and estates is the very reason for the creation of government.

In America, power comes from God to the individual and is loaned to the state. It does not belong to the state or a king. Religion has been a strong factor in preserving American civilization, through we have been careful not to establish a state religion. We took this idea, too, from Locke, who separated state from church, which had never been done before.

Locke was the originator of the idea that government must be strictly limited in power and function. He reached his position by reasoning that in a state of nature unprincipled forces could take away everything for which a person had worked or could work — even liberty and life itself. To protect against this, people created governments and gave them limited powers, primarily having to do with protection of "property," the name he gave to life, liberty and estates.

Thomas Jefferson was a disciple of John Locke. When he

wrote the Declaration of Independence, he drew liberally on Locke's writings and incorporated phrases into the document, the most famous of which is that men are "endowed by their Creator with certain unalienable Rights, that among these are Life, Liberty and the pursuit of Happiness." The Declaration only guarantees the pursuit, not the out come. Most of the Declaration, Stephens says, is a bill of particulars in an indictment of King George III. He had broken the contract of government with his people; therefore they not only owed him no allegiance, and they had a duty to replace his government with one which could protect their rights.

These precious rights have since been eroded as the "welfare state" attempted to guarantee results instead of opportunity. Congress, presidents and courts have loosened the limits on government and have weakened the protection of private property. The courts have allowed the taking of property rights without the compensation guaranteed in the Fifth Amendment to the Constitution. Powers guaranteed to the people and to the states have been assumed by the Federal Government. This has limited the opportunities of the people. It has made them poorer and less free.

One of the themes of the book is an interpretation of the Constitution. The authority for an act of Congress is in the Constitution and the Declaration of Independence. A logical place to find the intent of the Founders is in Locke, because they constructed a system of government based on his Second Treatise of Civil Government. Stephens makes a contribution by highlighting this.

The constitutionality of every bill introduced in Congress should be debated and established. For example, can the national government spend for public welfare? Madison and other Founders said it cannot, though the states may, and individuals clearly may spend all they want of their own money for it. In the 104th Congress, we introduced a bill which would require the citation of every constitutional authority for every law passed. That will undoubtedly be revisited in the 105th. If it eventually passes, the debates will be enlightening and will produce legislation which tends to conform more with our fundamental laws. Then, if the people want the Federal Government to perform functions not permitted under the Constitution, the amendment process is the proper way to consider them.

George Stephens points out that there has been a swing of the role-of-government pendulum approximately at the beginning of each century. There is no doubt that the 1994 election marked one such swing, as we enter the 21st century. It was a fundamental change, in which the people voted for opportunity and for a limited national government. This transformation was further ratified as voters in 1996 returned a Republican majority to Congress for the first time in sixty-eight years. The Contract with America and its legislative program, more than just the foundation for this change, were the means to secure the objectives and express the will of the people.

Newt Gingrich
Former Speaker of the
US House of Representatives

INTRODUCTION

Foundations and Failures of the US Government

Our Founders had the sound idea that government exists to protect property and preserve liberty, giving citizens the freedom to advance themselves through private contracts — but we lost confidence in that view just as the world began to emulate us. This book traces the process of winning and losing rights, explores the possibilities for restoration, and concludes that few reforms are likely to be adopted through politics.

We cannot govern ourselves nor secure our rights unless we understand our government's purpose, but many Americans do not. They tend to define the purpose variously as: to solve society's problems; to maintain order; to help the needy; or to spread wealth. It is none of these; instead, there is the unequivocal statement in the second paragraph of the Declaration of Independence that our government's function is to secure "life, liberty, and the pursuit of happiness" for its citizens. We tend to gloss over these words thinking, perhaps, that it is nice that the Founders wanted us to be happy. The words are not sentimental; they grant specific rights in property. Life and liberty are easily recognized properties, and the "pursuit of happiness" is a term that held an established meaning familiar to our Founders: the freedom to pursue a career and to enjoy the estate it creates. It is Thomas Jefferson's expanded version of John Locke's "life, liberty, and estates." Our civil rights are rights in property.

The property rights indicated are grounded in English Common Law and in the "natural rights" proclaimed by John Locke, the 17th-century English philosopher and the intellectual father of our country, in his *Second Treatise of Government.* He proposed a definition of the rights of citizens and the purposes of government, and America's founders a century later designed and created a government to protect them. To insure these rights, the Framers of the Constitution put in place various measures, and set specific limits on Congress's taxing and spending powers (limits nullified by the Supreme Court in 1936 but reaffirmed by it in 1995, as will be explained.)

According to Locke and our founding documents that flowed from him, one's rights in property must be respected, and, conversely, one must respect the property rights of others and may not damage their property in pursuit of one's own happiness. The guarantee of property rights for all is to be enforced by government. It is in this sense that "all men are created equal": equal before the law.

Many American histories and civics books do not identify government's purpose clearly. They do not acknowledge the Founders' passion for liberal, limited government, perhaps because many of the authors do not favor that kind of government. They therefore concentrate on other topics, such as Jefferson's "agrarianism," or the separation of church and state; first, we need a straightforward explanation of purpose and rights.

We must pass on our basic ideas of rights and freedom if our society and government are to survive. Our current direction leads toward the increasing chaos of government service to narrow interests. This book reviews the history of the principles upon which the US government was founded and their subsequent treatment, and says that if we follow Locke, the Declaration, and the Constitution, there will be more opportunity to pursue happiness, and the people will be more prosperous. The poor will benefit most, because they most need unrestricted opportunity before the law.

Lockean, limited government will be followed from the *Second Treatise* through Jefferson and the Declaration of Independence, the Constitution and its Bill of Rights, and through important US Supreme Court cases that have interpreted the principles of the founding documents. Reforms that would restore constitutional government are considered, and the US Supreme Court's recent efforts to reinstate it are described.

The Importance of Locke's Second Treatise

While there were many influences on our form of government, Locke's *Second Treatise of Government* was a strong one and provides an illuminating guide to the judicial interpretation of civil rights. To explain why government came into being, Locke began by picturing man without government, in a state of nature. There was a society, he suggested, but there was no common judge to settle disputes. It being impossible to enforce the laws of nature against the powerful and selfish, men made a contract between ruler and subjects, according the ruler certain limited powers to protect their property in exchange for their loyalty.

The Founders did not take their principles only from Locke or always directly from him; but they drew on Locke's spirit always and on his very words at times. They also looked to English Common Law, whose roots extended back to Rome and Greece. The Common Law principles had evolved over centuries; they were what worked for the benefit of people. (And when the English had a chance to secure freedoms, they took the opportunity: as with King John and the Magna Carta in 1215, the Petition of Grievances of 1610, and the English Declaration of Rights of 1689.)

According to Jefferson, in writing the early resolutions and the Declaration and the Constitution the Framers "rummaged" through Rushworth's compilation of English Common Law. Educated men in England and America in the early 18th century were familiar with *Cato's Letters*, which were in the spirit of Locke, criticizing government policy from a Whig (classical liberal) point of view; and Locke's own *Second Treatise* was a philosophical codification of the Common Law. Concerning the separation of powers, our Founders followed Montesquieu.

James Madison, "Father of the Constitution," insisted that the constitution crafted for the United States must be open to change only by amendment, and that is the procedure the Framers provided. If they had intended otherwise, there would have been no need to write a Constitution; like Great Britain's, the Supreme Law could have been ever-evolving from judicial interpretations and legislation, a "Common Law" constitution.

There is a passage in the *Book of Common Prayer*'s "Confession" which says: "We have left undone those things we ought to have done; and we have done those things we ought not to have done; and there is no health in us." The United States Government has often left undone things it ought to have done: effective protection of life, liberty, careers, and estates and the preservation of public order. Conversely, it sometimes has done things it ought not to have done: itself restricting liberty, taking property without compensation, requiring occupational licenses, ineffectively responding to criminal takings, and taking property from its citizens for unproductive and unconstitutional purposes. There is no health in that.

Government has undertaken many tasks which are properly matters of personal choice and of private contract, and which are therefore elements of the individual pursuit of happiness. It was not created to "do good" (except by protecting property), and many people have decided that it does good rather badly. As a result, their discontent has been growing. They have lost the trust they had in the federal government in the days when it protected them, and they seem to be looking for a model that limits government outside of its property protection functions. The one in the Declaration and Constitution is the best ever produced.

In any case, the Constitution is the Supreme Law. If we no longer agree with parts of it, we are obliged to amend it — not write the Common Law into it through the courts.

Cycles

In the history of the United States there have been roughly hundred-year-long swings in the US Supreme Court's and the public's view of the proper role of government and rights, and the legal treatment of rights in America has changed near the turn of each century. The 100-year periods are perhaps a function of the time it takes for judicial appointments to be made, and then for cases to work their way to the Supreme Court (which tends to decide narrowly and to change gradually). There is no natural or political law dictating the cycle. It is not deterministic, but it seems to have occurred. If it has, it may not continue, though a new cycle turning toward Locke may have begun on schedule near the end of the 20th century. This is no claim of an unbroken progression of Court cases toward or away from Locke in each of the cycles; rather, that there was an apparent trend. Some setbacks are noted.

The first "cycle" was a special case and lasted only 13 years. It began with the 1787 Constitutional Convention, which had adopted a closely-limited federal government. Immediately, Alexander Hamilton and his Federalist party began to depart from it — to expand the role of the national government and to limit individual rights.

Thomas Jefferson's Republicans campaigned to restore the limited-government concept of the Framers. When they won the election of 1800 on that platform, they initiated the hundred-year cycles; their view predominated through the 19th century. Then, at about the beginning of the 20th, under the Progressives (who sometimes thought of themselves as "Hamiltonians"), a dominant role for the federal government came into favor once more. The New Deal accentuated and accelerated it, "torturing" the Constitution (as one of its leaders put it) to fit its economic and property rights theories.

Senator Barry Goldwater's campaign for the presidency in 1964 foreshadowed change toward the Jeffersonian concept of govern-ment, though the public was not ready to follow and

Goldwater was soundly beaten. Ronald Reagan, while more conservative than libertarian, curbed some of the excesses of the "statism" (which is popularly called "liberalism" today) that had become the norm. In 1994 the congressional election was won on a platform called the "Contract with America," a document whose principles were individual liberty, economic opportunity, limited government, personal responsibility, and security at home and abroad — classically liberal in nature. The voters elected a majority of congressional candidates who supported the Contract.

The Contract's supporters issued a statement of principles, but in the traditional "conservative" manner only tried to modify "liberal" policy. They could have indicated another objective: to limit government to its constitutional functions; to reduce the budget and taxation to the level which would fund only the permitted functions — approximately 20% of current budgets. Probably, many of the Contract's supporters were not willing to go that far, though the public seemed inclined to move in that direction.

Historian Arthur Schlesinger, Jr. finds a cycle of about thirty years in which politics swings from "liberal" to conservative and back. Thomas Jefferson thought a revolution was needed every generation. Technology is changing the economy and society so fast that the political cycles may accelerate. Or the trend may be ever leftward, because there is always the temptation for interests to vote themselves money and power, and, absent limits, they can continue to do so.

This book tracks the cycles and inquires what are our chances of restoring our government to its intended role; few reforms, I think, are likely to be achieved through politics.

Supreme Court Restoring the Constitution

The US Supreme Court is the surest way to reform, because it has recently restated our principle of limited government, and it is settled tradition that we abide by the verdicts of the Court. The book concludes by noting that the Supreme Court began the restoration by declaring in 1995 that we have a limited government and that Congress has only the few powers granted it in Article I, Section 8; and (in 1994) that it will scrutinize property rights as strictly as other rights such as freedom of speech. The people will have better, more efficient help through the private sector and the charities of a remarkably compassionate people, which will be better funded because people are more lightly taxed. State governments can provide a "safety net." At the same time, less help will be needed because more jobs will be created by the investment money that remains in private hands. The increasing incidence of investment in business through individual ownership of stock, pension funds and other forms of business property will generate important political support for the Court. People will want their investments protected.

It may take much of a century to complete this process, if completed it will ever be, but because of the Supreme Court the outlook for liberty and constitutional government at the beginning of the 21st century is more encouraging than it has been for many years.

1. The Spirit Of American Rights

Restrictions on Government

Government, as noted, has a very limited, very important purpose: to secure the freedom to create and enjoy property and to preserve life and liberty. Our Founders adopted this concept of John Locke, who explained the role of government in society in his *Essay Concerning the True Original, Extent and End of Civil Government*.

Because of his devotion to Locke, Thomas Jefferson not only drew on the *Essay* as a source of ideas but quoted and paraphrased it in the Declaration of Independence. The rights of men to "life, liberty, and the pursuit of happiness" was Jefferson's version of Locke's "life, liberty, and estates" — which Locke called "property." Pursuit of happiness is broader because, in addition to an estate, it covers a career through which to create an estate and to build a life around it, but both men's definitions of property meant to guarantee happiness to citizens through the freedom to make their own choices in life while allowing others to do the same.

In the state of nature, Locke reasoned, the enjoyment of property is uncertain and constantly exposed to the invasion of others, so it can only be guaranteed by the contract of government. "The great and chief end, therefore, of men's uniting into commonwealths, and putting themselves under government, is the preservation of their property, to which in the state of nature there are many thing wanting.

"First, there wants an established, settled, known law, received and allowed by common consent to be the standard of right and wrong, and the common measure to decide all controversies between them. For though the law of nature be plain and intelligible to all rational creatures; yet men being biased by their interest, as well as ignorant for want of study of it, are not apt to allow of it as a law binding to them in the application of it to their particular cases.

"Secondly, in the state of nature there wants a known and indifferent judge, with authority to determine all differences according to the established law. For everyone in that state being both judge and executioner of the law of nature, men being partial to themselves, passion and revenge is very apt to carry them too far, and with too much heat, in their own cases; as well as negligence and unconcernedness to make them too remiss in other men's.

"Thirdly, in the state of nature there often wants power to back and support the sentence when right, and to give it due execution. They who by any injustice offended, will seldom fail, where they are able, by force to make good their injustice. Such resistance many times makes the punishment dangerous, and frequently destructive, to those who attempt it.

"Thus mankind . . . are quickly driven into society, (and) . . .

take sanctuary under the established laws of government, and therein seek the preservation of their property."

Locke's writings were known and admired by virtually all educated people at the time of the founding of the United States of America. Though his treatise was designed to make government the protector of the people, he felt it necessary to warn, at the outset, of its inherent dangers: "Political power, then, I take to be a right of making laws with penalties of death, and consequently all less penalties, for the regulating and preserving of property, and of employing the force of the community in the execution of such laws, and in the defence of the commonwealth from foreign injury, and all this only for the public good." Then he described the principles of a government circumscribed in powers but adequate to protect life, liberty and estates.

To reduce the dangers, the Framers those who drafted our Constitution limited the kinds of laws our government may make. For example, criminal penalties may only be imposed by a court; Congress may not pass a bill of attainder penalizing an individual without trial; government may not take a citizen's property without just compensation, and only for a public purpose. Still, the ability to seize at gunpoint and to imprison the non-payer of taxes and the breaker of regulations is real power. One may think it is of no consequence to oneself what laws are made, because one will never commit a felony; but it is of considerable consequence when one may be escorted by armed guard over a misdemeanor violation of an occupational licensing or zoning law and may be killed, legally, for resisting (whether in fact or in the fancy of the arresting officer).

The laws that may be passed, therefore, are restricted to those which protect "life, liberty and the pursuit of happiness." The Constitution has a Bill of Rights to protect property (including speech, freedom of assembly, and other forms of property), and it has a General Welfare clause enumerating the few taxation and spending powers necessary to maintain a general government to protect property.

Such a government's functions do not include export loans, business aid, medical insurance, housing, education, food stamps, job training, crop subsidies, the arts, social security, or the other functions of the modern "welfare state." This type of government could be authorized by constitutional amendment, but it has not been.

The restrictions on Congress's powers were generally upheld for more than a century; they began to change in the late 19th century, and were breached drastically in a Supreme Court opinion in 1936 which said that Congress's taxing and spending was not to be limited by the direct grants of legislative power found in the Constitution. The Court found instead that the "Welfare" clause (part of Article I, Section 8, which restricts the taxing and spending by Congress) is a grant of unlimited power. Other laws of that era further eroded the restrictions, as will be explained.

The 1936 opinion was in error. The Framers intended strict limits. There can be no other explanation of why they wrote a constitution instead of allowing it to evolve (as in the United Kingdom and many other nations). Their unwillingness to provide legislative free rein instructs us that Congress's taxing and spending powers are meant to be limited to the enumerated functions. Surely, they did not swelter through the hot Philadelphia summer of 1787, putting restrictions on government only to insert a

General Welfare clause that would undo all of their previous careful drafting (as the Supreme Court opined in 1936).

Their intent could be demonstrated through close study of the evolution of the Common Law in England and America before 1776, but it can be done more conveniently with the help of Locke, whose writing was based upon that very body of Common Law. We can reasonably say that when our laws are in concert with Locke's philosophy, they are probably what the Founders intended; otherwise, they are not.

Locke's Contributions to Our Form of Government

Locke's two major contributions to political thought were: 1) to show that individual freedom and protection of rights in property are the purpose of government; and 2) to make the state entirely secular, with all church functions divorced from it. His ideas were not new. They traced back to Greece and Rome, to the Magna Carta, and to the religiously tolerant Levellers in the time of his youth. The *Second Treatise* was partly original thought by John Locke and mostly a philosophical codification of English Common Law.

Classical economist and political philosopher Friedrich Hayek notes that:

> John Locke's *Second Treatise on Civil Government* . . . has come to be known mainly as a comprehensive philosophical justification of the Glorious Revolution; and it is mostly in his wider speculations about the philosophical foundations of government that his original contribution lies. Opinions may differ about their value. The aspect of his work which was at least as important at the time and which mainly

concerns us here, however, is his codification of the victorious political doctrines, of the practical principles which, it was agreed, should thenceforth control the powers of government.

Philosopher Thomas Hobbes provided reasons for men to obey kings, and he had given the church a secondary role in the state but had not freed the state from it. He thought the king should have complete control of the state's policy. His *Leviathan,* in 1651, ostensibly a political essay, was an ecclesiastical discussion in part. In contrast, Locke believed that religious struggles were not the state's concern and wanted to free it from them. After his writings, English political theorists did not often diverge from his view of the proper relationship between church and state, and his perspective was written into our Bill of Rights in the First Amendment.

Hobbes said that men are by nature equal in bodily and mental capacities, in the sense that an individual can compensate for his deficiencies in one respect by his other qualities (this opinion foreshadowed modern discussions about equality of results in life versus equality of opportunity). He believed that men were selfish and tended to live in a state of war with each other (in the "nature" of war, if not actually fighting it), and that the only way they could live together is under the state, with all power conceded to a dictator. Locke, like St. Francis of Assisi, believed that men had good in them, were not completely selfish, and that they could live in a society which existed independently from the state. His belief in the essential goodness of men made him believe that they could govern themselves.

Despite their differences, both Hobbes and Locke started from the state of nature to explain why the political state came into being. In Locke's view, the laws were not to be given by any ruler. People were rational beings who could discover certain laws of nature with which to govern, and because they were rational they were capable in their search for security and pleasure of governing themselves according to those laws. People were equal in rights and duties; but he did not suggest that they had equal abilities.

In the state of nature there was a society, but there was no judge to settle disputes. Since each man individually could not enforce the laws of nature against human predators, men made a contract to set up a state. Through this contract, the subjects give the ruler (their state) power only so that their own welfare is increased and their property protected in a way not possible in the state of nature, where it may be taken away by selfish, unprincipled forces. If the ruler keeps the contract, the subjects owe him their loyalty. Under this contract of government, all political power is a trust for the benefit of the people, and the people themselves are at once the creators and beneficiaries of that trust. The state is to be concerned only with public order: those aspects of behavior which have to be regulated for the protection of the public's lives, liberty and estates.

It was Thomas Jefferson's passionate belief in these ideals that led him to base the powers of government on "inalienable rights." Most of his Declaration of Independence is an indictment of King George III for his failure to keep the contract with his American subjects. He had broken it, and it was therefore void. The members of the Second Continental Congress, representing the states, edited and signed Jefferson's draft.

That Locke's was not the sole mind behind our system is

illustrated by the fact that he was rather vague about the organization of government, an important subject in the Constitution. He said that the legislative and executive power "come often to be separated." The clear establishment of legislative, executive, and judicial powers and their separation in our governmental tradition came from Montesquieu's *The Spirit of Laws*. Locke thought that the legislature should be supreme among the branches, that it should provide for judges, and that the judges should review laws. The power to make war and treaties he called "federative." He said that everyone must submit to the majority, or there would be no compact of government.

Citizens were presumed to agree to obey their rulers on condition that their natural rights were respected, and these rights were considered to come not from the rulers but from God. Men could not take them away; they were "inalienable" — but Locke had no illusions that this notion would protect us. He thought that men should revolt against a ruler who failed to respect natural rights. The Declaration of Independence asserted this against King George, and Jefferson echoed it in his later statement that a little revolution was good every generation. What he actually seemed to advocate was periodic, reasoned revision, so that government could catch up with technological and social change.

This does not mean that the Supreme Court has been justified in changing the Bill of Rights by judicial fiat. It may be changed only by constitutional amendment. New laws are needed for new times, but they must be judged by the principles of the Constitution. The rights of the citizens do not change.

The right to private property was the fundamental law of nature, according to John Locke. In a state of nature man could claim land only if there was enough left for others; and he had no right to more goods than he could consume before they spoiled. With the advent of money there was no such practical restriction, but Locke still felt that a man should leave a share for others, that there should be no monopolies. (Keep in mind that land is only one form of property, so here we are exploring only the land subset of Locke's property philosophy.)

"Ever since a court had laid down in the famous Case of Monopolies that the grant of exclusive rights to produce any article was 'against the common law and the liberty of the subject,' the demand for equal laws for all citizens became the main weapon of Parliament in its opposition to the king's aims," said Friedrich Hayek. It was another kind of economic regulation, however, that occasioned the first great statement of the basic principle. The Petition of Grievances of 1610 was provoked by the king's new regulations in London and his prohibition against the making of starch from wheat. This celebrated plea of the House of Commons states that, among all the traditional rights of British subjects,

> . . . there is none which they have accounted more dear and precious than this, to be guided and governed by the certain rule of law, which giveth to the head and the members that which of right belongeth to them, and not by any uncertain and arbitrary form of government . . . Out of this root has grown the indubitable right of the people of this kingdom, not to be made subject to any punishment that shall extend to their lives, land, bodies, or goods, other than such as are ordained by the common laws of this land, or the statutes made by their common consent in parliament.

It was, finally, in the discussion occasioned by the Statute of Monopolies of 1624 that Sir Edward Coke, the great fountain of Whig principles, developed his interpretation of the Magna Carta that became one of the cornerstones of the new doctrine. In the second part of his Institutes of the Laws of England, soon to be printed by order of the House of Commons, he not only contended (with reference to the Case of Monopolies) that "if a grant be made to any man, to have the sole making of cards, or the sole dealing with any other trade, that grant is against the liberty and freedom of the subject, that before did, or lawfully might have used that trade, and consequently against this great charter"; but he went beyond such opposition to the royal prerogative to warn Parliament itself "to leave all causes to be measured by the golden and straight mete-wand of the law, and not to the uncertain and crooked cord of discretion."

The Special Importance of Property Rights

Property rights are uppermost in Locke's scheme of government, and by property he meant whatever one can create with one's own labor. He wrote that " . . . every man has a property in his own person. This nobody has any right to but himself. . .", and he went on to reason that one creates additional property by working for it. "The labor of his body, and the work of his hands, we may say, are properly his. Whatsoever, then, he removes out of the state that Nature hath provided and left it in, he hath mixed his labor with it, and joined to it something that is his own, and thereby makes it his property. It being by him removed from the common state Nature placed it in, it hath by this labor something annexed to it that excludes the common right of other men. For this labor being the unquestionable property of the laborer, no man but he can have a right to what that is once joined to, at least where there is enough, and as good left in common for others." He said that: " . . . of the products of the earth useful to the life of man, nine-tenths are the effects of labor; nay, if we will rightly estimate things . . . we shall find that in most of them ninety-nine hundredths are wholly to be put on the account of labor," so that not only the landed gentry have rights in property; everyone has. This obviously creates incentive to work and be productive.

Libertarian Charles Murray writes:

> No form of behavioral freedom can exist without a foundation of property rights.
>
> Because property rights are so easily dismissed as something mostly involving rich people and real estate, it is important first to emphasize how pervasive property rights are. Technological innovation and the entertainment industry depend on intellectual property rights in the form of patents and copyrights, for example. But even when it comes to physical property, everyone's daily life depends on property rights. Imagine, for example, a world in which there are no property rights whatever; nobody can say of anything that he owns it. The result would be the law of the jungle. You would have no legal right to refuse to let a stranger come in off the street and walk off with your television, no right to complain to the police if the same stranger takes food from your plate. The legal force behind your right to lock the door of your home against an intruder depends on your property rights in the lock and the door. Nor does this state of affairs change if you rent your home; a rental agreement has meaning only

insofar as it conveys property rights, delimited in extent and time, from the owner to the renter.

Property rights are a way of distinguishing between thine and mine. They are the material by which even the humblest person can demarcate the sphere within which he makes the decisions. Without property rights everything else falls apart . . .

Knowing that something is yours makes it your responsibility. Ownership is a way to bring out the best in human beings. Property rights are a basis not only for human freedom but also for careful stewardship.

Locke's labor theory of property rights was used by classical economist Ricardo to arrive at his labor theory of value. It was later twisted into socialist and communist theory in the sense that those doctrines claimed to make labor paramount; but in practice they left out property rights and made government paramount.

James Madison explained that property

. . . means that dominion which one man claims and exercises over the external things of the world, in exclusion of every other individual . . . it embraces everything to which a man may attach a value and have a right; and which leaves to every one else the like advantage. In the former sense, a man's land, or merchandise, or money, is called his property. In the latter sense, a man has a property in his opinions and the free communication of them. He has a property of peculiar value in his religious opinions, and in the profession and practice dictated by them. He has property very dear to him in the safety and liberty of his person. He has an equal property in the free use of his faculties, and free choice of the objects on which to employ them. In a word, as a man is said to have a right in his property, he may be equally said to have a property in his rights.

Note that Madison, following Locke, placed freedom of speech and religion among rights in property. The New Deal Supreme Court, which reckoned property rights to be worthy of less protection than free speech rights, should have placed property rights on at least an equal plane, because speech rights are an element of them.

Locke's doctrine meant that one's property was not to be alienated by any other person, nor was one to damage or take anyone else's property — and that restriction extended to the state. Our Founding Fathers realized that the state would have to take property for certain public purposes, but required that the owner be left whole — having been provided compensation.

Locke's view of property was practical, inclusive, and liberal. It is the essence of political freedom. Who can argue that a man does not have a property in his own person — for who else could have it? To argue that a man does not have a property in his person is to argue for slavery. Locke believed that government could take the fruits of one's labor and intellect only in the case of a compelling public need and with compensation, and then only through due process of law. A person was free to contract away his property, or any of his several rights in it, for gain. Virtually everything was to be done by private contract, therefore not through government. The contract with government was only to protect private contracts, and the government was not entitled to any of the gains therefrom.

Individuals are capable of restricting others' rights to some extent, but not nearly to the same degree as government. It was necessary to organize government only to protect property and, once it was organized, other freedoms had to be protected against government's power. Locke wrote in the *Second Treatise* that "men unite in a society for the mutual preservation of their lives, liberties, and estates, which I call by the general name 'property'."

He said that the supreme power (the legislative) cannot take from any man any part of his property without his consent (the preservation of property being the end of government and that for which men enter into society) He noted that for the protection of government everyone should pay his share, but only with the consent of the majority.

The tax system Locke advocated was a fee for the protection of life, liberty and estates: the same proportion of each person's wealth — a flat tax. He noted that "It is true governments cannot be supported without great charge, and it is fit everyone who enjoys his share of the protection should pay out of his estate his proportion for the maintenance of it . . . But still it must be with his own consent — *i.e.*, the consent of the majority, giving it either by themselves or their representatives chosen by them; for if anyone shall claim a power to lay and levy taxes on the people by his own authority, and without such consent of the people, he thereby invades the fundamental law of property, and subverts the end of government. For what property have I in that which another may by right take when he pleases to himself?" (This is why redistributionist taxation is an illegal taking of property, as is regulatory taking without compensation. They are prohibited by the Constitution, which specified taxing powers only for property protection and a few general government functions.)

To illustrate this principle, Locke noted that while a sergeant can command a soldier to stand in the mouth of the cannon and face almost sure death, he cannot command the soldier to give him one penny of his money, nor can the general — who can condemn him to death for desertion — "dispose of one farthing of the soldier's estate, or seize one jot of his goods, because the commander has his power for the preservation of the rest (peoples' property), but the disposing of his goods has nothing to do with it."

Of the judicial system and punishment, Locke said that:

> Man being born, as has been proved, with a title to perfect freedom and an uncontrolled enjoyment of all the rights and privileges of the law of Nature, equally with any other man, or number of men in the world, has by nature a power not only to preserve his property; that is, his life, liberty, and estate, against the injuries and attempts of other men, but to judge of and punish the breaches of that law in others, as he is persuaded the offense deserves, even with death itself, in crimes where the heinousness of the fact, in his opinion requires it.

And he noted that, in a political society, this power is

> resigned into the hands of the community, and the community comes to be umpire . . . and decides all the differences that may happen between any members of that society concerning any matter of right, and punishes those offenses which any member hath committed against the society with such penalties as the law has established.

Liberals and Conservatives

That is a summary of John Locke's philosophy of government and rights, the spirit of which is embodied in the fundamental law of the United States of America. The purpose of our government is freedom and the protection of property. The people who subscribed to the doctrine were and are liberals, because the word is derived from the Latin word *liber*, "free." Now they are called "libertarians," because "liberal" has been wrongly applied to those who believe in a large measure of state control and who are in truth "statists," or "democratic socialists."

Philosopher-economist Ludwig von Mises said, in *Human Action*, that he

> . . . [employed] the term "liberal" in the sense attached to it everywhere in the nineteenth century and still today in the countries of continental Europe. This usage is imperative because there is simply no other term available to signify the great political and intellectual movement that substituted free enterprise and the market economy for the pre-capitalistic methods of production; constitutional representative government for the absolutism of kings or oligarchies; and freedom of all individuals from slavery, serfdom, and other forms of bondage.

The Lockean, libertarian, classical-liberal philosophy should not be confused with conservatism which, as Friedrich Hayek observed, " . . . may succeed by its resistance to current tendencies in slowing down undesirable development, but, since it does not indicate another direction, it cannot prevent their continuance. It has, for this reason, invariably been the fate of conservatism to be dragged along a path not of its own choosing. The tug of war between conservatives and progressives can only affect the speed, not the direction of contemporary development."

2. JOHN LOCKE: FOUNDER OF THE FOUNDERS

Locke's Place Among Philosophers of Government

Most Americans know a few things about Jefferson, Adams, Madison, Washington and other Founders, but few know John Locke, from whom those men took much of their political philosophy. Professor Harold Laski wrote that Locke is "taken for granted, rather than read." His ideas so permeate our world that we believe in them without knowing that they are his. We regard them as ours — our tradition — our right. But Americans should know him better.

A number of thinkers, stretching from Plato and Aristotle to Blackstone and including Thomas Aquinas, Grotius, Pufendorf, Rousseau, Montesquieu, Hobbes, and others, made contributions, but this political and social philosopher influenced the author of the Declaration of Independence and the Framers of the Constitution more than any other.

There have been other important theories of social institutions besides Locke's. One school, in which David Hume and Bernard

Mandeville were important figures, stresses an evolution of ideas — that social and political systems developed almost accidentally — that nations adopted the ideas that worked, rather than developing them rationally, and indeed this is how the English Common law evolved.

As Hayek describes it:

> . . . we have had to the present day two different traditions in the theory of liberty: one empirical and unsystematic, the other speculative and rationalistic — the first based on an interpretation of traditions and institutions which had spontaneously grown up and were but imperfectly understood, the second aiming at the construction of a utopia, which has often been tried but never successfully. Nevertheless, it has been the rationalist, plausible, and apparently logical argument of the French tradition, with its flattering assumptions about the unlimited powers of human reason, that has progressively gained influence, while the less articulate and less explicit tradition of English freedom has been on the decline . . . But we must not forget that the political conclusions of the two schools derive from different conceptions of how society works. In this respect the British philosophers laid the foundations of a profound and essentially valid theory, while the rationalist school was simply and completely wrong.

Mandeville demonstrated that self-interested individuals produced an overall order that was beneficial to them — akin to the "invisible hand," Adam Smith's metaphor for the guidance of the marketplace in economics. Hume argued that, though a set of obligatory moral principles cannot be demonstrated, the moral order is not necessarily arbitrary.

These writers believed that the evolution of social institutions was independent of design, and that they were not based on God's dispensation. In contrast, Locke believed that a rational system of law could be discovered from the laws of Nature. He did, however, acknowledge the effect of legal evolution when he wrote in respect to "*iure divino*" (divine law), if its supporters meant by it ". . . that the sole, supreme, arbitrary power and disposal of all things is and ought to be by divine right in a single person, 'tis to be suspected they have forgot what country they are born in, under what laws they live, and certainly cannot but be obliged to declare *Magna Carta* to be downright heresy. . . ." In other words, there was a huge debt to English Common Law, as well as to intellect. He was the philosopher of the Common Law.

What matters for the people of the United States of America is that their governing principles derive primarily from John Locke and English Common Law — and less from the other philosophers. Locke's principles and the Common Law are written into the Declaration of Independence and the Constitution, especially in its Bill of Rights. They are the foundation of the supreme law of our land, so the laws passed under it must reflect his principles, and judicial interpretation must give deference to them.

Even those who do not agree with Locke must abide by his principles, if they believe in the rule of law. If they are not willing to do that, they must start over with a new Declaration and Constitution, or if they disagree with parts of them they must propose amendments. We are all, *volo nolo*, disciples of Locke.

Locke's Life

Born in Somerset, England in 1632, Locke went to Westminster School in London and to Christ Church, Oxford in

1652. He obtained a fellowship there in 1658, the year Oliver Cromwell died and the unrest began that was to lead to the Restoration of the king in 1660. In a parallel with our own time, sports and entertainment were paramount, and scholarship had been forced into a secondary role under the Royalists. In spite of this, he studied Latin, Greek, and Hebrew, as well as rhetoric, logic, and mathematics.

He was educated in philosophy and medicine, and in 1666 he became physician to Lord Ashley, the future Earl of Shaftesbury and minister to the crown. He worked for Ashley as tutor to his son, lived in his household, and became his political advisor.

Locke's fame in history rests mostly on his political and social philosophy, but the breadth of his learning is illustrated by the fact that he was also a fine medical scientist. Thomas Sydenham, the greatest British physician of his time, with whom Locke worked, said that Locke had amongst the medical men of his time few equals and no superior. The two advanced the cause of medical research in a project to determine the cause of smallpox. He also operated successfully on Shaftesbury's life-threatening brain tumor. He inserted a silver tube to prevent the healing of the wound and allow the poisons to drain off. His patron's life was probably extended by many years as a result.

In Ashley's household he wrote his essays, beginning with the one on Toleration. His "Essay Concerning Human Understanding" grew out of meetings he held with small circles of friends to discuss philosophical topics. He suggested that they ought to consider the extent and limits of man's understanding itself (serious people, these). While he was quite modest about the essay, Voltaire, Diderot, Rousseau and others accepted it as their guide and referred to him as the "greatest of all philosophers" since Plato, the "sage," a creator of metaphysics comparable to Newton, the creator of physics. He himself was enough of a scientist to become a member of the Royal Society and of its executive committee.

He was not a drudge. James Gibson said that he had a genius for friendship, and this helped him create the discussion circles. Those who knew him stressed his kindliness. He was modest, quiet and unassuming, but he could laugh heartily.

In 1667 Locke was appointed secretary to Sir Walter Vane, ambassador to the Prussian court in Brandenburg, and in 1672 Secretary of Presentations under Shaftesbury, who had become Lord Chancellor. The post of Secretary of the Council of Trade and Plantations came a year later.

Shaftesbury fell out of favor with the king in 1675, and Locke himself went to France for his "health" after writing a pamphlet critical of the royal policies, which was condemned by the government and burned by the hangman. He stayed in France for four years. In 1681, Shaftesbury was charged with treason and imprisoned in the Tower of London because he was involved in the unsuccessful campaign to prevent James II, the Roman Catholic, from succeeding his brother, Charles II. Shaftesbury supported the Protestant Duke of Monmouth. He was acquitted of the treason charges and exiled to Holland, where he died in 1683.

Locke went to Holland late that year, apparently just ahead of difficulties with the authorities — so quickly that he could not make financial arrangements or even pack his clothes. Around this time Locke wrote "An Essay Concerning the True Original, Extent and End of Civil Government," the famous *Second Treatise of Government* — the work which most influenced the United States.

(His *First Treatise* refuted Sir Robert Filmer's argument that the rights of royalty were inherited from Adam.) He stayed for five years, writing and enjoying Holland's political and religious toleration, and returned when King James was overthrown and William and Mary succeeded to the throne. In fact, he accompanied Queen Mary to England from Holland in February, 1689.

Shaftesbury had been one of the Lords Proprietors of Carolina, and in 1699 Locke contributed to or perhaps wrote all of "The Fundamental Constitutions of Carolina." It created a serfdom, antithetical to his other writings, whereas the sections on religious toleration sound like him. One wonders if he was ordered to write the untypical part, or if perhaps he did not write it.

King William wanted Locke to be ambassador to the court at Brandenburg, where Locke had experience, but he declined the post for reasons of health, as he declined other foreign service positions. In 1696 he became a member of the Board of Trade and Plantations and was its most influential member until his death in 1704.

3. LOCKE ON EDUCATION AND RRELIGIOUS TOLERANCE

His Essays

John Locke did not publish any essays in English until 1690, when he was 58, though his "Letter Concerning Toleration" had appeared in Latin, in Holland. This does not mean that he developed his ideas late in life. He had thought them out many years earlier and had made notes in his commonplace book. The first draft of "An Essay Concerning Human Understanding" was done as early as 1671. "An Essay on Toleration" was written, but not published, five years earlier. It included the central ideas of the "Letter Concerning Toleration" and the "Two Treatises on Civil Government."

The *Second Treatise of Government* is, to Americans, the most important of his essays, because our theory of rights was developed in it; but his ideas on education and religion are significant as well. The ones on religious tolerance are echoed in our founding documents, and all of the essays reveal the depth and breadth of his thinking. They also illustrate his belief in the importance of families and their guidance to children, so he speaks to those concerned with social life and morals.

The Establishment of Locke's day believed that certain ideas are innate, but he thought that we are born in ignorance and that even our theoretical ideas of identity, quantity, and substance are derived from experience. He said: "The senses at first let in particular ideas, and furnished the yet empty cabinet." Then the mind abstracts theoretical ideas, and so "comes to be furnished with ideas and language, the materials about which to exercise its discursive faculty."

He also thought that we receive signals both from within and without ourselves, but we have no way of knowing which come from without so we cannot test their authenticity. Thus, man must settle for probable knowledge.

The traditional view was that some sort of moral knowledge was innate, but Locke did not agree: God had given men a faculty of reason and a sentiment of self-love; these combined to produce morality. Reason could discern the principles of ethics, or natural law, and self-love should lead men to obey them. For Locke, Christian ethics was natural ethics. The teaching of the New Testament was a means to an end — happiness in this life and the next. The teachings of the Gospel, for example loving God and one's neighbors, were to be followed not just because Jesus said so, but because they promoted one's happiness.

Educational Theories

Locke shocked the educational establishment of his day with "Some Thoughts Concerning Education," because the establishment was accustomed to the educational rituals handed down from the Middle Ages. He attacked schools where "Latin and learning make all the noise," and where "education fits us rather for the university than the world." He believed that some practical training is needed to fit a man for his place in the community, and that Greek, Latin, grammar, rhetoric and logic should not be taught exclusively. Most of his educational ideas were adopted in the next century and a half. The pendulum swung so far in the mid-20th century toward practical education (specialized training, rather than liberal arts) that there was support for less fitting of the child to the community (or worse, support for moral relativism: fitting the societal standards to the child's ethnic or social group). He did, however, insist that a child should be considered an adult in the making, and that education be varied with the individual.

A healthy body was necessary for a sound mind, and he gave suggestions on play, sleep and clothing. He was a progressive educator in that he thought that a child learns best by doing, and that if studying is made a game a child's interest in the work increases and learning is hastened. Pictures should supplement printed words, and teachers should note aptitudes and encourage them. It may seem surprising that a bachelor should have so many ideas about child development, but he was tutor and companion to the Earl of Shaftsbury's children, who were devoted to him, and, as always, he was observant and thoughtful.

He said that very young children should be taught to be civil to "inferiors" and to be kind to animals, because it is a short step from cruelty to animals to inhumanity to men. Civility to "inferiors" is important, because if one is polite to those one considers inferior, one will be polite to all. In the early 21st century, civility is markedly missing, and if children were receiving the parental guidance specified by Locke, society would doubtless work much better.

Locke believed children should be praised for good behavior and that shaming them should be the main form of discipline. Corporal punishment was to be restricted to cases of "stubbornness, lying, and ill-natured actions."

A child should be taught absolute obedience and awe for his parents in his early years, but when he has learned to reason, discipline should be relaxed and he should be treated more and more as an adult. "The sooner you treat him as a man, the sooner he will be one." Then friendship should replace authority.

He eliminated logic, rhetoric, Greek, and much grammar, suggesting that while the child is young, he should learn one foreign language — by conversation and not by mastering the rules of grammar. The careful study of grammar should be confined to English. (Would that it now extended even to English!) Latin should be taught the same way as the foreign language, and Greek should be taught only to future scholars (though John Adams and Thomas Jefferson learned both ancient languages and sometimes wrote to each other in them). A son should have virtue, worldly wisdom (which will help in life), breeding, and learning. The latter is important only if it contributes to a life that is useful and pleasant. Breeding and virtue may seem quaint, in our time, but breeding is what a mother is teaching when she sends a child off to visit, saying, "Remember who you are!" Virtue connotes absolute, not relative, standards of conduct. One "lifestyle" may not be as good as another. There are Eternal moral standards.

He scorned ivory-tower scholars who talk "with but one sort

of men and read but one sort of books. They canton out to themselves a little Goshen in the intellectual world where the light shines . . . but will not venture out into the great ocean of knowledge."

Locke's Views on Religion

Locke was very religious, and he decided to stay in the Anglican Church rather than side with the Dissenters because he objected to their insistence that they alone held the key to salvation more than he objected to the Church's hierarchy and connections to the government. He did not give up his plans to enter the ministry until he was in his thirties.

He believed that God had sent his Son to reveal his true nature as a merciful God, rather than the vengeful, harsh one of the Old Testament. Even if men failed to live up to the moral code of the New Testament, they could have salvation through God's grace. He criticized dogma and ritual, as Christ had criticized it when He said that the plethora of religious laws were not important, and that "[the first and great Commandment is:] thou shalt love the Lord thy God with all thy heart and all thy soul, and the second is like unto it: thou shalt love thy neighbor as thyself." This is echoed in his concept that one must grant to others the same rights he enjoys.

At Oxford, Locke came to know the Latitudinarians and their religious tolerance. Later, when the young man was made secretary to Sir Walter Vane, ambassador to the Prussian throne at Brandenburg, he found further religious tolerance and noted that it promoted political and economic unity. Shortly thereafter he wrote his "Essay Concerning Toleration," but did not publish it. He wrote the "Letter Concerning Toleration" in 1685 in Holland, and by that time English thinkers had found the idea of religious toleration good for their country, based on Holland's experience.

He distinguished between the requirements for a voluntary association in a religion and of a state. Church members do not give up the rights that they cede to a state, because they may quit the religion. The only power a church has over them is to expel them for not abiding by its precepts. The state may compel compliance up to and including the penalty of death.

Too often, he found, when church and state are closely tied, the state decides on the teachings of the church instead of the church guiding the morals of the state. There was ample evidence of that in the founding of the Anglican Church and decreeing of its teachings by Henry VIII when the Church of Rome would not let him divorce and remarry.

John Locke argued that no one can ever know all the truth about religion. The persecutor may be in error and the persecuted correct. No one has the right to force his views on another when the views cannot be proved by reason. This is especially indefensible when the religion is based on love and charity for others, as in Christianity. It would be useless to force one's religious viewpoint on others. Religion is a matter of faith and cannot be promoted at the point of a gun.

There were two exceptions to his religious tolerance: atheists and Papists; atheists, because they have no moral basis for their judgments, and Papists because they owed their allegiance to a foreign ruler and were intolerant; but he did not advocate restriction of their civil rights because of their religious beliefs.

Our rights of free speech, press, and assembly stem at least in part from the "Essay Concerning Toleration" and the later "Letter Concerning Toleration." The Supreme Court now refuses to uphold limitations upon the freedoms guaranteed in the First Amendment unless particular speeches, written matter, or assemblies and demonstrations constitute a "clear and present danger" such as the overthrow of our government (Justice Holmes' test), or to an immediate, overt act of lawlessness. Thus, the Court has adopted Locke in its First Amendment interpretations, while in respect to rights in property, it has abandoned him in spite of the fact that he demonstrated that securing those rights is the reason for instituting government.

4. Jefferson: Locke's Disciple

A Brief Biography

John Locke's doctrines were already the basis of American provincial documents, but Thomas Jefferson and the Second Continental Congress embedded them in the nation's founding document, the Declaration of Independence, and he is used here to represent the Founders, as their intellectual leader. Jefferson was thoroughly versed in Locke and included him with Newton and Bacon in his "trinity of immortals." In the Declaration are nearly-verbatim quotations, and he followed the philosopher's principles of government throughout his political career.

Thomas Jefferson was a well-educated man of good family background who graduated from the College of William and Mary, America's second-founded institution of higher learning. He was from Albemarle County in the Virginia Piedmont, and although he came from an aristocratic, propertied family, his politics always reflected respect for the yeomanry that predominated in his area.

After college, he studied law under eminent Williamsburg

lawyer George Wythe, one of the best political and legal minds in Virginia and a classical scholar in spite of his lack of formal education. Even as a law student, young Jefferson participated in discussions with the leading politicians in the capital and with royal governors Fauquier and Botetourt. He was 23 when he began the practice of law in Williamsburg, and he continued in it for seven years.

When Governor Botetourt took office, he dissolved the Assembly and issued writs for the election of a new one. The freeholders of Albemarle County elected Jefferson one of its two burgesses. He was in the House of Burgesses when it supported Massachusetts in opposing the Townshend duties and when they declared that they, not Parliament, had the right to levy taxes on the Colony. As a result of these actions, the Governor dissolved the Virginia legislature. The members immediately went into rump session at a tavern, where they signed a non-consumption and non-importation agreement concerning British goods. But, loyal British subjects that they were, they then drank toasts to the King and the Governor. Botetourt called new elections and most of the same men were elected. His Excellency did not enforce any penalties.

In the year he entered the Legislature, Jefferson began to build Monticello. His marriage to the widow Martha Wayles Skelton, on New Year's Day, 1772, gave him a reason to hasten the work, which actually went on for the rest of his life.

In 1774 the Virginians gave moral support to the "Boston Tea Party." The Committee of Correspondence, of which Jefferson was a member, ordered that letters be sent to committees of correspondence in the other colonies proposing that a general congress should be called.

Jefferson's principal biographer Dumas Malone says that the young statesman went through "an evolutionary rather than a revolutionary process, and that with him thought long preceded action and determined its direction in advance." Even during his practice of law he "read politics" and concentrated on the history of legal doctrines and institutions, certainly including Locke's. John Adams, in old age, wrote him that the real revolution in America was likewise "in the minds of the people" between 1760 and 1775, before a drop of blood was shed at Lexington.

Jefferson's Beliefs

Malone also notes that the doctrine of natural rights was one of Jefferson's postulates. As early as 1770, he had said publicly that under the law of nature all men are born free. He knew Locke's phraseology by heart in 1776, when he incorporated it into the Declaration of Independence (with George Mason's "pursuit of happiness" substituted for Locke's "estates"). He had not copied much from the philosopher's writings into his notebooks, but that was probably because he was already so familiar with them. He took Locke's ideas for granted, as did his contemporaries.

He was convinced that men were born to freedom because of natural rights. He said "The God who gave us life gave us liberty at the same time." Nothing less could have been expected of God, for liberty was right, just as force was wrong. Malone notes that he was not a cynic and never ceased to believe that good, not evil, lay at the heart of the universe; and it was this faith that kept him from being a mere intellectual and gave his leadership a spiritual quality. It should also be recalled that his "immortal" hero Locke believed in the essential goodness of man.

Later, Jefferson was to write to Abigail Adams: "The spirit of resistance to government is so valuable on occasion that I wish it to be always kept alive. It will often be exercised when wrong, but better so than not to be exercised at all"; and to another correspondent: "God forbid we should every twenty years be without such a rebellion! What signify a few lives lost in a century or two? The tree of liberty must be refreshed from time to time with the blood of patriots and tyrants. It is its natural manure." (In private, he sometimes used flamboyant language he did not use in public.)

While in Paris, Jefferson wrote: "And we think ours a bad government (under the Articles of Confederation)! The only condition on earth to be compared with ours is, in my opinion, that of the Indians, where they have still less than we. The European [versions], are governments of kites (hawks) over pigeons. The best schools for republicanism are London, Versailles, Madrid, Vienna, Berlin." To George Washington he wrote that he had become many more times an enemy of monarchy since coming to Europe. "There is scarcely an evil known in these countries which may not be traced to their king as its source, nor a good which is not derived from the small fibres of republicanism existing among them. I can further say with safety, there is not a crowned head in Europe whose talents or merits would entitle him to be elected a vestryman by the people of any parish in America."

From Montesquieu he got the idea that the right of suffrage is fundamental to a democratic government. He was convinced that aristocracies of birth and wealth were artificial and unjust; the aristocracy in which he believed was one of talent and virtue.

Lord Dunmore, then Governor of Virginia, dissolved the Assembly in 1774 — and at the next election got the same men for his pains, so he prorogued it and did not permit it to convene for a year. The same burgesses held a rump convention in Williamsburg. Jefferson could not be there because of ill health, so he was not elected a delegate to the General Congress in Philadelphia. He did, however, send a set of resolutions based on Locke's natural rights, which was to be moved as instructions to the Virginia delegates. It was not acted on officially, but it was printed as *A Summary View of the Rights of British America* (not his title). It soon was published in Philadelphia and twice in England, and it contributed greatly to his reputation.

In the *Summary View* he noted that the ancestors of Americans had been free and self-governing in England, just as their Saxon forefathers had been free in the wilds. This gave his position historical precedent as well as philosophical authority. He said that the colonists had fought for themselves and had the right to hold onto what they had, and that they thought proper to adopt that system of laws under which they had hitherto lived in the mother country, and to continue their union with her by submitting themselves to the same common Sovereign, who was thereby made the central link connecting the several parts of the empire thus newly multiplied.

He then made points that formed the basis for the Declaration of Independence two years later: that there was a contract between the people of the colonies and the King, formulated in the early charters. He emphasized the restrictions these documents placed on royal powers and did not regard the charters as gifts. He also claimed free trade with the world as a right of the colonies. His most startling statement was that: "The true ground on which we declare these acts void is, that the British parliament has no right to exercise its authority over us." The heights to which eyebrows were raised in London can be imagined.

He noted a series of usurpations of power by Parliament, including suspension of New York's legislature, saying: "One free and independent legislature hereby takes upon itself to suspend the powers of another, free and independent as itself; thus exhibiting a phenomenon unknown in nature."

In the *Summary View* he asserted that the colonies desired to abolish slavery (which turned out not to be the case when he tried to put similar language into the Declaration of Independence). He noted that Virginia's previous attempts to prevent the importation of slaves from Africa had been vetoed by the King.

He made another statement that must have seemed radical to Englishmen and especially to the King: that "Kings are the servants, not the proprietors of the people. Open your breast, sire, to liberal and expanded thought. Let not the name of George the Third be a blot in the page of history."

While the *Summary View*'s language was not as artful as that to come in the Declaration, he ended with ". . . the God who gave us life gave us liberty at the same time. . ."

The Continental Congress did not adopt his statement, though it proclaimed that the provincial assemblies had the exclusive right of taxation and policies concerning the colonies, subject to the King's veto. It agreed that Parliament could regulate external commerce.

In March 1775 a convention was held in Richmond to which Jefferson was a delegate. Patrick Henry made his "Give me liberty, or give me death" speech there, and he urged defensive measures. A committee was established to plan for a militia, and Jefferson was appointed to it. The most important happening at the convention concerning Jefferson was that it elected him alternate to Peyton Randolph in the Continental Congress. As it happened, Randolph had to return home, and Jefferson went to Philadelphia to make history.

The Revolution Begins

About a month after the convention in Richmond had adjourned came the news of the battles of Lexington and Concord. Governor Dunmore called the Assembly into session to present conciliatory proposals from Prime Minister Lord North, and Jefferson attended, before going to Philadelphia.

Dunmore had removed powder belonging to Virginia that was stored in the Williamsburg magazine. The burgesses objected so strongly to the governor about it that he feared for his safety, joined his family on board a British warship, and conducted his business from there — which made him ineffective thereafter.

Jefferson drafted a reply to Lord North to the effect that any colony that contributed to the defense of the Empire and to the support of its own government should be exempt from British taxation. This was rejected. The committee's final objection said: "We consider ourselves as bound in honour, as well as interest, to share one general fate with our sister Colonies; and would hold ourselves base deserter of that union to which we have acceded, were we to agree on any measures distinct and apart from them." They were presenting themselves as Americans as well as Virginians.

The treasurer of Virginia sent with Jefferson the expense money for its delegation at the Continental Congress. It was raised by subscription, not from taxes, and Jefferson had made his own contribution. On the trip to Philadelphia he had to contend with different currencies in Maryland, Delaware and Pennsylvania, which helps explain why, a few years later, the states decided that some aspects of the union needed to be changed.

Shortly after his arrival in Philadelphia, and after the battle of Bunker Hill, Jefferson and a large crowd saw General Washington off to Boston. Then, the sixty or so delegates met and deliberated through a hot summer. Jefferson, not a good speaker, remained silent on the floor, though he made useful contributions to committee work.

New Englander John Adams said that the Virginian seized upon his heart and that he had brought with him a reputation for "literature, science, and a happy talent for composition." They began a historic friendship, soon cemented in work on the Declaration of Independence, reinforced in their joint mission to Paris, sundered in presidential politics, and renewed for their lifetimes in retirement until they both died on the 50th anniversary of the signing of the Declaration of Independence.

John Dickinson of Pennsylvania and Thomas Jefferson drafted a "Declaration upon Taking up Arms." As usual, the Virginian spoke of compacts freely made. He wrote, and it was included:

> Our forefathers, inhabitants of Great Britain, left their native land to seek on these shores a residence for civil and religious freedom.
>
> . . . our attachment to no nation upon earth should supplant our attachment to liberty.

Not included was:

To ward these deadly injuries from the tender plant of liberty which we have brought over, and with so much affection fostered on these our own shores, we have pursued every temperate, every respectful measure.

We have supplicated our king at various times, in terms almost disgraceful to freedom, . . .

. . . to preserve that liberty which he (our Creator) committed to us in sacred deposit.

He was kept busy writing. Because of his reply to Lord North for the Virginia House of Burgesses, he was asked to draft a similar one for the Continental Congress. He was well aware that the colonies were in a state of war, and that the differences would be settled on the battlefield and not through negotiations. His friend John Randolph had moved to England. In a letter to him, Jefferson spoke his mind about the King, calling him "the bitterest enemy we have. . . ." Then he said: "Believe me, dear Sir, there is not in the British empire a man who more cordially loves a union with Great Britain, than I do. But by the God that made me, I will cease to exist before I yield to a connection on such terms as the British Parliament propose; and in this, I think I speak the sentiments of America."

He returned home before the end of the session. In the next one, he would draft the Declaration of Independence.

5. Jefferson, Locke, And
The Declaration Of Independence

Prelude to the Declaration

Jefferson missed the opening of the next session of the Continental Congress: his wife was ill, his mother died, and he himself was ill for five weeks. Since each state had only one vote, which could be cast by all or any of its delegates, it was not critical which ones were there, anyway.

He returned to his lodgings at Graff's house in Philadelphia, having sounded out local sentiment before he left home and been convinced that nine-tenths of the people favored independence. He received a letter from his old friend, John Page, who said: "For God's sake declare the colonies independent and save us from ruin." Another friend wrote that the notion of independency had spread fast and that he thought it would be adopted in the current session of Congress.

The Virginia Assembly instructed its delegates to propose to Congress that the united colonies be declared free and independent states. The resolution lay upon the table in

Philadelphia, while Virginia created a new government and hoisted a new flag. Jefferson drafted and sent to Williamsburg a constitution including a list of charges against George III, which was attached to the constitution as a preamble. The Virginians declared that, because of the acts of misrule enumerated by Jefferson, the government of their country as exercised under the Crown was totally dissolved, foreshadowing the more famous action about to come.

> *In Congress, Friday, June 7, 1776.* The delegates from Virginia moved in obedience to instructions from their constituents that the Congress should declare that these United colonies are & of right ought to be free & independent states, that they are absolved from all allegiance to the British crown, and that all political connection between them & the state of Great Britain is, & ought to be, totally dissolved; . . .

— this is from Jefferson's notes, published in his autobiography. The resolution was presented by Richard Henry Lee.

It is remarkable that one of Jefferson's recommendations was that colonies established from Virginia territory west of the mountains should be free and independent of that colony and all the world. Similar provisions were included by other states and by acts of Congress, so that this provision paved the way for consistent governance of the expanded republic. Future Americans were to enjoy the same benefits. The original states, in Jefferson's view, must not repeat the mistakes of Britain.

There was debate over the resolution, but not agreement, and it was decided to postpone the decision until July 1. A committee consisting of Jefferson, John Adams, Benjamin Franklin, Roger Sherman and Robert Livingston was appointed to prepare a declaration. The group met at Franklin's house, where he was confined with the gout, and discussed the general form the declaration should take. Jefferson, known to be a good writer, was asked to draft it.

Richard Henry Lee said that the Declaration had been "copied from Locke's treatise on government." While that was the philosophical source, Jefferson used two principal models in his drafting. One was his own preamble to the Constitution of Virginia; the other was George Mason's draft of the Virginia Declaration of Rights; and both were descendants of the English Declaration of Rights of 1689.

Jefferson's draft constitution for Virginia included the charges against the King that he put into the Declaration of Independence. Mason's Declaration proclaimed:

> (1) That all men are born equally free and independent, and have certain inherent natural rights, of which they cannot, by any compact, deprive or divest their posterity; among which are life and liberty, with the means of acquiring and possessing property, and pursuing and obtaining happiness and safety.

> (2) That all power is vested in, and consequently derived from, the people; that magistrates are their trustees and servants, and at all times amenable to them.

> (3) That government is or ought to be instituted for the common benefit, protection, and security of the people, nation or community. Of all the various modes and forms of government, that is best which is capable of producing the greatest degree of happiness and safety, and is most effectually secured against the danger of maladministration; and that, whenever any government shall be found inadequate or contrary to these purposes, a majority of the community hath an indubitable, unalienable and indefeasible right to reform, alter or abolish it, in such manner as shall be judged most conducive to the public and the Colonies; and

such is now the Necessity which constrains them to alter their former Systems of Government. The History of the present King of Great Britain is a History of repeated Injuries and Usurpations, all having in direct Object the Establishment of an absolute Tyranny over these States. To prove this, let Facts be submitted to a candid World.

The Indictment of George III

Without Locke's and Jefferson's statements of rights, what follows in the Declaration might appear to be only a quarrelsome list of complaints against the King. It is, rather, a bill of particulars in an indictment of King George III for his failure to keep the contract with his American subjects. He had broken the contract, and it was therefore void. This shows that, from our government's inception, contract has been fundamental to our system. It *is* the system. There is a contract between the people and their government to preserve life, liberty and the pursuit of happiness; other affairs are a matter of private contract.

> He has refused his Assent to Laws, the most wholesome, and necessary for the public good . . .
>
> He has forbidden his Governors to pass Laws of immediate and pressing importance . . .
>
> He has refused to pass other Laws for the accommodation of large districts of people, unless those people would relinquish the right of Representation in the Legislature, a right inestimable to them, and formidable to tyrants only . . .
>
> He has dissolved Representative Houses repeatedly, for opposing with manly firmness his invasions on the rights of the people . . .
>
> He has . . . , He has . . . , He has . . . , He has combined with others to subject us to a jurisdiction foreign to our

constitution, and unacknowledged by our laws; giving his Assent to their Acts of pretended Legislation: . . .

The bill of indictment continues:

For imposing Taxes on us without our Consent . . .

For depriving us in many cases of the benefits of Trial by Jury . . .

For taking away our Charters, abolishing our most valuable Laws and altering fundamentally the Forms of our Governments . . .

For suspending our own Legislatures, and declaring themselves invested with power to legislate for us in all cases whatsoever. [The "all cases whatsoever" was intolerable to Jefferson and the colonists.]

He has abdicated Government here, by declaring us out of his Protection and waging War against us.

. . . He has excited domestic insurrections amongst us, and has endeavored to bring on the inhabitants of our frontiers, the merciless Indian Savages, whose known rule of warfare is an undistinguished destruction of all ages, sexes and conditions.

In every stage of these Oppressions We have Petitioned for Redress in the most humble terms: Our repeated Petitions have been answered only by repeated injury. A Prince, whose character is thus marked by every act which may define a Tyrant, is unfit to be the ruler of a free people. Nor have We been wanting in attention to our British brethren. We have warned them from time to time of attempts made by their legislature to extend an unwarrantable jurisdiction over us. We have reminded them of the circumstances of our emigration and settlement here. We have appealed to their native justice and magnanimity, and we have conjured them by the ties of our common kindred to disavow these usurpations, which would inevitably interrupt our connections and correspondence. They too have been deaf to the voice of justice and consanguinity. We must, therefore, acquiesce in the necessity, which denounces our Separation, and hold them, as we hold the rest of mankind, Enemies in War, in Peace, Friends.

The reference to "merciless Indian Savages" may seem insensitive in our day, but the British incited the Indians to attack from the west while British regulars and Tories fought on the coast.

Independence!

The Declaration concludes, in the words of Congress's own July 2 resolution, composed by Richard Henry Lee of Virginia:

> We, therefore, the Representatives of the UNITED STATES OF AMERICA, in General Congress, assembled, appealing to the Supreme Judge of the world for the rectitude of our intentions, do in the Name and by authority of the good People of these Colonies, solemnly publish and declare, That these United Colonies are, and of right ought to be FREE AND INDEPENDENT STATES; that they are Absolved from all Allegiance to the British Crown, and that all political connection between them and the State of Great Britain, is and ought to be, totally dissolved; and that, as Free and Independent States, they have full Power to levy War, conclude Peace, contract Alliances, establish Commerce, and to do all other Acts and Things which Independent States may of right do.
>
> And, for the support of this Declaration, with a firm reliance on the protection of Divine Providence, we mutually pledge to each other our Lives, our Fortunes and our sacred Honor.

It was signed by President of the Continental Congress, John Hancock, and the delegates.

Congress retained his: " . . . we mutually pledge to each other our Lives, our Fortunes and our sacred Honor." Thus, the signers pledged their own property (lives, fortunes) to secure these benefits for their fellow citizens. Locke did not include honor among the parts of property. He didn't have to — in his and in Jefferson's day it was the most cherished and respected attribute a gentleman had.

One of Jefferson's strong complaints was that the King permitted the slave trade. He condemned him for violating the "most sacred rights of liberty" in doing so, but the clause was omitted by the Congress in order to preserve the unanimity of the states against England. His fellow Virginians had included abolition of the trade in the preamble to their constitution, as he wrote it, though they did not outlaw it. South Carolina and Georgia favored continuance of the traffic, and some Northerners did not want it stopped because they were in the slave-shipping business. Jefferson believed that slavery was in conflict with the higher law of Nature, but he was never able to abolish it and he kept his own slaves.

Independence was declared on July 2nd (and John Adams thought that was the day that would be celebrated). On July 4, twelve states agreed to the Declaration of Independence and signed it. New York did not do so until July 15. In the meantime, it was printed and circulated.

There was no celebration of that Fourth of July in Philadelphia. The Declaration of Independence was proclaimed on the 8th by the local Committee of Safety in the State House yard in the presence of a large crowd. Jefferson was there, but not in the spotlight (as doubtless he did not so wish to be).

Cheers resounded; there was a parade on the Commons; bells

rang all day and into the night. The ties with Great Britain had been cut, and there was a new nation in the world: the United States of America.

6. LOCKE IN THE CONSTITUTION

Shortcomings of the Articles of Confederation

It is probable that every Framer of the Constitution was familiar with John Locke's writings. They had classical educations, which included study of his writings. Many were attorneys. The principles and words of the Constitution and especially its Bill of Rights show that they had Locke's doctrines very much in mind, even if the Common Law was the more direct antecedent.

They wrote a new governing document to replace the Articles of Confederation, because the States that had declared themselves independent of Great Britain tended to act as though they were independent of each other, too. It was the style to refer to one's state as "my country." And yet, they were engaged in a war against a common enemy.

The Articles of Confederation had stipulated: "The said states hereby severally enter into a firm league of friendship with each other," but the Confederation could not collect taxes, pay the public debt or encourage and regulate commerce. General

Washington had a very difficult time maintaining an army. It was short of powder, food, clothing, medicine and barracks. Congress sent requisitions for funds to the states, but often they did not receive the money. The states that paid were angry with the ones that did not. James Madison of Virginia rebuked Oliver Ellsworth at one point in the Convention by pointing out that Connecticut had refused to pay its share.

Alexander Hamilton, Washington's *aide-de-camp*, pressed the General for strong measures, and in 1780 Hamilton wrote a letter to a friend saying that it was impossible to govern through thirteen sovereign states and that the only remedy was to call for a convention of all of them. He publicized the need for it over the next seven years, and in 1782 he got the New York legislature to pass a resolution urging one be convened. With the end of the war, the states were even less cooperative, but a dispute between Maryland and Virginia over navigation of the Potomac River led to a meeting in Annapolis in 1786, opening a door to resolution.

After the Convention, Hamilton explained in *The Federalist*, No. XXX, that "the government of the Union has gradually dwindled into a state of decay, approaching nearly to annihilation."

The Annapolis Commission recommended to Congress that all thirteen states appoint delegates to convene at Philadelphia the next May, "to take into consideration the trade and commerce of the United States." Commerce was a real problem, because states imposed duties on each other. From our vantage point it is difficult to imagine paying tariffs on goods manufactured in another state. The farmers of western Massachusetts were in rebellion against the money interests in Boston. The Annapolis report suggested that the whole federal system needed attention.

The Constitutional Convention of 1787 —
Debating a New Form of Government

There was no thought of writing a new constitution, because there was little political support for a strong national government. Congress agreed that a convention was needed, however, and resolved that it was to meet "for the sole and express purpose of revising the Articles of Confederation." James Wilson, in the Convention debate on the Virginia Plan(favoring the large states) versus the New Jersey Plan (favoring the small states), said that he thought the Convention was authorized to "conclude nothing, but to propose anything"; and that is the attitude the delegates took.

There were 74 delegates named to the Convention, of which 55 attended. John Adams and Thomas Jefferson were not there. Adams was envoy to London, and Jefferson was the Confederation's representative in Paris. The Bostonian's recent book on constitutions was being circulated among convention members, and Jefferson had sent, at his friend Madison's request, every book he could find that was related to the subject — hundreds of them. Madison was a man who prepared and who kept careful records. It was to be he, not the official secretary, who took detailed notes of the proceedings, and he attended every session.

The delegates worked in secrecy, and it is well that they did because it allowed uninhibited discussion of controversial and complex issues. If the states ever call another convention, it will probably operate under the glare of publicity and with hourly statements to the press by members. Lobbyists and pressure groups will be in the galleries and halls, and one wonders if a document of the quality of our Constitution can emerge.

As the delegates approached their task, they knew that Locke considered the legislative power to be supreme. He said in *Of Civil Government*:

> The great end of men's entering into society being the enjoyment of their properties in peace and safety, and the great instrument and means of that being the laws established in that society, the first and fundamental natural law, which is to govern even the legislative itself, is the preservation of the society, and (as far as will consist with the public good) of every person in it. This legislative is not only the supreme power of the commonwealth, but sacred and unalterable in the hands where the community have once placed it.

They were in the same Pennsylvania Statehouse as in 1776, with the Natural Law again at the center of their deliberations; they understood that it was imperative to create a sound legislature. Many of them were doubtless drawing on experience in their states and in England, all of which reflected the Lockean model.

Locke left to others the decisions on unicameral or bicameral legislatures: "Though the legislative, whether placed in one or more (house), whether it be always in being or only by intervals, though it be the supreme power in every commonwealth . . . ." Obviously, Locke had experience with legislatures that sat continuously (like our modern Congress) but he was open to other options. Eight states had two houses, while the Congress had only one.

Locke said that legislators "are themselves subject to the laws they have made; which is a new and near tie upon them to take care that they make them for the public good." (Two hundred years later the Congress they created was routinely exempting itself from its own laws. The first action of the 104th Congress in 1994 was to place itself under the laws it made.)

Those were some of the principles available from Locke — or from the existing legislatures founded upon them — to guide the Framers. Among procedures for the Convention, they adopted a rule that made decisions non-binding, with the result that as the issues were worked out, members could change their minds, accommodate to new understandings and work toward a complete concept of government.

The Virginia Resolves were introduced at the outset of the Convention. They had been drafted by the seven delegates from that state (probably led by James Madison) and, while drastically amended over the summer, they formed the basis for discussion. They proposed a new, *national* government, with its own executive, legislature and judiciary. The legislature was to have two branches, the first (the representatives) to be elected by the people, and the senators to be elected by the first branch. This was radical; the Convention had been instructed only to amend the Articles of Confederation, but the Virginians believed that a new model was needed, and they were from the most populous, most influential state.

The initial Lockean influence showed in the adherence to the belief that government should protect life, liberty and estates. While the United States had won the revolution as a confederation of autonomous states, it had been a close thing, and the government very nearly had not been able to preserve the liberties of its citizens. Therefore, a closer union was necessary. People do not need to be steeped in the ideas of Locke to want security, of course; but Locke reflected universal values in his Natural Law, so his ideas and the people's desires meshed easily.

Many Americans think that the Convention established a

"democracy," but that word conjured up visions of unruly mobs, like Captain Shays and his rebellious farmers from western Massachusetts. The word was in somewhat better odor with the Jeffersonians a few years later, but it continued to carry very negative connotations among the High Federalists led by Alexander Hamilton. The 1787 Convention was mainly concerned with organization of a government to preserve property. Locke's doctrines entered the Constitution most specifically in the Bill of Rights adopted by Congress and the states following the Convention.

The Organization of Government

Edmund Randolph got right to the heart of the question of organizational structure when he said that "a national government consisting of a supreme legislative, and of executive and judicial (branches)" was needed. There was stunned silence. Did the Convention propose to overthrow state governments? The meanings of "federal," "national," and "supreme" were debated at length. They were exploring federalism, without a model.

Madison observed that a federal government operates on states, while a national one operates directly on individuals. James Wilson pointed out that if the operation was on states, then a state of 10,000 people would have the same power as one of 40,000. How could the states (which were creating the national government) and the people of the nation at large both be represented fairly? Much of the debate during that sweltering summer was about how to resolve that question.

Locke had been somewhat vague on the optimal organization

of government but had noted that the legislative and executive powers are often separated in governments. The experience incorporated into the language of the Virginia Resolves derived from the practice of the states (which had been national governments, in effect), informed by Montesquieu's model of separate executive and legislature — so that is the model that was proposed.

Locke acknowledged the need for an executive, in order "to see to the execution of the laws"; and he pointed out the need for "federative" power to act in foreign relations. The Framers accorded this power to the executive, with ratification power in the Senate and foreign affairs appropriations in the House of Representatives.

The proposal that there be a single executive was controversial because it smacked of royal governors. If there should be such an entity, some members of the Convention wanted it accountable to the legislature. Some wanted a plural executive. And some wondered whether he ought to be allowed an "executive negative," a veto power.

The first item of governmental organization to be agreed on was that the legislature should have two branches; next, that the House of Representatives be popularly elected. It was then agreed that provision should be made for the admission of future states into the Union. (Though Jefferson was not in attendance, many delegates recalled that he had proposed that future states have the same powers as the existing ones, in his resolution offered by Virginia in Congress, June 7, 1776. As mentioned above, he had said that colonies established from Virginia territory west of the mountains should be free and independent of that colony and all the world).

The question of suffrage in election of the House came up

again — should the members be elected by the people or by the states? In the case of direct election, some delegates were afraid of deleterious influence by those without property. (As Catherine Drinker Bowen noted, in *Miracle at Philadelphia*, poverty in those days was synonymous with indigence.) There was plenty of land, and labor was scarce — so that anyone in poverty must be slothful. The holding of property had good connotations. Indeed, the Revolution had been fought for its protection.

The Great Compromise on Legislative Representation

The most vexing question, politically, was how to apportion power between large and small states. As to the wisdom of investing authority in "the people", Hamilton gave a five-hour address, early in the Convention, in which he made his views clear. "Can a democratic Assembly, who annually revolve in the mass of the people, be supposed steadily to pursue the public good?" He favored the British model of a single executive, elected for life, which would put the executive above corruption. This formula came close to monarchy. He wanted to annihilate state distinctions and state operations — to have a general and national government, completely sovereign.

His proposals were not even discussed. After the speech he went home to New York, and seldom returned to Philadelphia; and yet, in 1936, his notions about unlimited taxing and spending powers for Congress were taken as authority by the Supreme Court over those of Madison, who attended all of the sessions, took the authoritative notes, and who said that the Convention had intended that the powers be strictly limited to those it granted in

Article I, Section 8.

It had been agreed that representation in the House of Representatives would be proportioned to population (the Virginia Plan) and that gave the larger states a decided power advantage. The New Jersey Plan, for equal representation of the states, was preferred by the small states. Its principal feature was that the states voted equally in a Congress with a single house that could legislate on limited matters. The powers derived from the states, not from the people. It proposed a plural executive.

The Convention was deadlocked. They could not even agree on where to look for inspiration. Luther Martin read passages from Locke, which the delegates said was not necessary — they all knew his texts and had fought for the principles in them. Benjamin Franklin proposed prayer each day to help resolve their problems, saying: "I have lived, Sir, a long time, and the longer I live, the more convincing proofs I see of this truth — that God governs in the affairs of men." But they did not have the prayers, because they could not afford a chaplain.

Connecticut now advanced Ellsworth's previously-proposed "Great Compromise," under which the states would have equal voice in the Senate while retaining proportionality in the House of Representatives. Madison was adamantly opposed, because he wanted to follow the plan of equal representation of citizens. So did many other delegates.

The other two members of the New York delegation quit and followed Hamilton home. Luther Martin said, "We were on the verge of dissolution, scarce held together by the strength of an hair, though the public papers were announcing our extreme unanimity." Washington wrote to Hamilton, "I almost despair of seeing a favorable issue to the proceedings of the Convention, and do therefore repent of having had any agency in the business."

The Great Compromise was adopted as the only way around the deadlock, and the crisis was averted. The large states were not happy, but there was no way to go on without it.

Now the largest questions had been answered. The Committee of Detail then divided what had been agreed so far into articles and sections, and had the draft of the work to date printed.

First Draft of the Constitution

The draft provided for a national government of specifically-enumerated powers, a government directed at the people as individuals rather than at the states, carefully naming the national government's powers.

Congress had the power to pass navigation acts, collect taxes and imposts, and regulate commerce among the several states. There had been a question as to whether Congress or the states would control the slave trade. Here, in particular, the South and the North had different interests, as their economic bases were industry in the North and agriculture in the South. Congress won jurisdiction over the slave trade, as it held control of other forms of commerce, but a compromise was reached for purposes of representation and taxes: slaves would be counted in the proportion of five for every three white inhabitants.

The Southern states conceded that the importation of slaves would cease in 1808. Locke had said, under the heading "Of Slavery" in the *Second Treatise*, that:

> The natural liberty of man is to be free from any superior power on earth, and not to be under the will or legislative

authority of man, but to have only the law of nature for his rule. The liberty of man, in society, is to be under no other legislative power but that established, by consent, in the commonwealth, nor under the dominion of any will, or restraint of any law, but what the legislative shall enact, according to the trust put in it . . . not to be subject to the inconstant, uncertain, unknown, arbitrary will of another man.

Jefferson believed that the institution of slavery was wrong and violated the rights of man, and he tried to abolish the slave trade in a statement included in the preamble to the Virginia Constitution, and as a provision in his draft of the Declaration of Independence — though he realized that abolition was not politically possible. The Convention delegates wanted to keep all thirteen states in the Union, but South Carolina and Georgia would not stay if slavery were abolished. Other southern states were divided in opinion, and there were slave-trading interests in the New England maritime industry as well. In any case, the Convention's task was to create a workable government, and Congress could make laws on slavery when the time came.

The question would not be resolved in their time. The terrible American Civil War, two generations later, was fought because a nation that professed to believe in Locke's Natural Rights for all men could not live the lie that some men were property. Lincoln used Jefferson's *Declaration* to mobilize the people to abolish slavery. After that war, the Thirteenth, Fourteenth, and Fifteenth Amendments were added to he Bill of Rights. They outlawed slavery; barred the states from abridging the privileges and immunities of citizens of the United States, or depriving any person of liberty and property without due process of law, or denying to any person within their jurisdiction the equal protection of the laws; and extended voting rights to all citizens. These Amendments adopted John Locke's views on slavery and demonstrated that his ideas concerning rights were as compelling in 1865 as they had been one hundred years earlier.

In 1787, the members of the Convention agreed on the length of terms to be served and the citizenship requirements for holding office. The delegates remained true to Locke when they said: "But no religious Test shall ever be required as a Qualification to any Office or public Trust under the United States," though officers were required to take an oath to support the United States Constitution.

They also resolved that Congress could establish a ten-mile square Federal District. Jefferson later compromised with Hamilton, agreeing with him that the national treasury should take over the states' war debts in return for locating the Federal District on the Potomac, next to Virginia, rather than in New York, Philadelphia, or elsewhere.

The draft constitution gave Congress the "power to lay and collect taxes," and the "power to regulate commerce with foreign nations, and among the several states." (Roger Pilon of the Cato Institute notes that this meant "to regularize"; to assure that the states put up no barriers — rather than a writ for Congress to regulate all trade). And Congress could establish post offices, mint and borrow money and set up judicial tribunals.

A controversial provision was "to subdue a rebellion in any state on the application of its legislature; to make war; to raise armies; to build and equip fleets." Some delegates did not believe the national government should have to wait for a state legislature's invitation to quell rebellion; others felt strongly that it should.

The military provisions were made in order to protect life, liberty and the pursuit of happiness, which the Framers understood to be the primary purpose of government, and their understanding reveals the irrelevancy of the sometimes-heard argument that the budgets of the National Endowment of the Arts or certain social welfare programs are only equivalent to the cost of an aircraft carrier or of a nuclear submarine and therefore should not be eliminated. The military expenditures are legal; the social ones are not.

One difficult subject was the number of states necessary to ratify this very instrument of government that was being crafted. Technically, what the Convention was doing was amending the Articles of Confederation, which would require unanimity; but Wilson propounded the view that only states that ratified would be bound by the new Constitution. That view was accepted, and the number to ratify was fixed at nine.

Should ratification be by the legislatures, or by the people in state conventions? Here, the vote was in favor of the people, because legislatures are creatures of state constitutions and cannot be greater than their creators. The people, Madison said, "were in fact the fountain of all power."

The Final Draft

The wordsmiths of the Committee of Style and Arrangement took responsibility for honing the final draft; they began the document with the unheard-of "We the People of the United States . . . " (which upset Patrick Henry and others who thought that the union should be one of states) "in Order to form a more perfect

Union, establish Justice, insure domestic Tranquility, provide for the common defence, promote the General Welfare, and secure the Blessings of Liberty to ourselves and our Posterity, do ordain and establish this Constitution for the United States of America."

The Framers had spent a summer working to organize a government whose purpose was to protect life, liberty, and the pursuit of happiness. Now "the Plan" was being established on behalf of the people.

Adoption, Without a Bill of Rights

The Plan was almost complete, and there was no bill of rights. George Mason urged that one be added as a preface and suggested that it could be prepared in a few hours from state declarations. He had written Virginia's, and eight states had them (all derived from Locke and English Common Law). Some thought that the state bills of rights would suffice, but Mason pointed out that the new Constitution would be paramount and needed its own.

The vote was ten states to none against adding a bill of rights, which seems astounding today because the rights guaranteed in the first ten amendments have assumed such importance. The Framers, however, believed that liberty was firmly in place, inviolate, and did not need reiteration. Their mission was to organize an effective government.

Alexander Hamilton asked: "Why declare that things shall not be done which there is no power (in Congress) to do?" Roger Sherman said: "No bill of rights ever yet bound the supreme power longer than the honeymoon of a new married couple, unless the rulers were interested in preserving the rights; and in that case they have always been ready enough to declare the rights, and to preserve them when they were declared. . . ." These were prophetic words in light of the many instances in which the plain words and intent of the Bill of Rights have been misinterpreted and ignored in the last seventy years.

Some of the members then expressed themselves in favor of a second convention, to be held after the states had the opportunity to make their preferences and objections known. Others said that there would be so many opinions that nothing would be decided, and we can imagine that there was little enthusiasm for going through the difficult exercise again. A motion for a second convention was voted down unanimously.

"On the question to agree to the Constitution as amended. All the States, 'Aye'." Their labors were over. On September 17, 1787 a majority of all of the state delegations present agreed, and the state delegates who were still there and who agreed to it, signed.

It was printed in newspapers immediately, and it occasioned surprise, happiness, shock, dismay, and much debate by the public. Richard Henry Lee of Virginia, who had been elected to the Convention but who had refused to serve because he was a member of Congress and would have to pass on it, said that it was "highly and dangerously oligarchic" and that: "Either a monarchy or an aristocracy will be generated." The objections of dissenting members of the Convention were published.

The *Federalist Papers*, by Madison, Hamilton and Jay, were printed in the New York press: they were well-reasoned, intellectual expositions of the need for the new form of government.

Edward Gaylord Bourne, in his introduction to *The Federalist*, calls them "among the political classics of the world . . . and the best single presentation in moderate compass of the ruling ideas of political philosophy of the eighteenth-century Whigs as applied to the problem of securing in a government both liberty and efficiency."

Jefferson wrote Madison from his diplomatic post in Paris: "I like much the idea of framing a government which should go on of itself peaceably without needing a continual recurrence to the state Legislatures. I like the organization of the government into Legislative, Judiciary and Executive . . . . I will now add what I do not like. First, the omission of a bill of rights." He thought that the states would reject the Constitution and force inclusion of a Bill. The states did force it — but without rejecting the Constitution. Later he wrote that "The example of changing a constitution, by assembling the wise men of the State, instead of assembling armies, will be worth as much to the world as former examples we have given them. The Constitution . . . is unquestionably the wisest ever yet presented to men."

The matters of most concern to the public were the lack of a bill of rights and the power of Federal taxation.

Ratification

Members of the Convention who were members of Congress hurried to New York. Eight days after it received the Constitution, Congress recommended that the states call ratification conventions. Delaware ratified first, on December 6. Several states, especially Pennsylvania, Massachusetts and Virginia, had bruising battles in convention. The delegates from the western extremities of these and other states tended to be fearful of the proposed national government, because with its broad powers over the regulation of commerce and over foreign relations Congress might negotiate away their navigation rights to the Mississippi to appease Spain.

Edmund Randolph announced in Virginia's ratification convention that he had been in favor of previous amendments (*i.e.*, for a bill of rights at the beginning of the Constitution). He was now for subsequent amendments and was for the Constitution. It was a big breakthrough, because he had proposed the Resolves that had been the basis of the constitutional debate (though it may have been Madison who drafted them). Virginia ratified on June 25th and included a Declaration of Rights in twenty articles, proposed by Patrick Henry. Ten of them, in simplified form, were enacted by the first Congress and ratified by the states.

When New Hampshire became the ninth state to ratify, the new government came into existence. New York ratified on July 26th, 1788. In its 1787 convention North Carolina had refused to ratify until there was a bill of rights, and when there was one, in 1789, it joined the union. Rhode Island had not sent delegates to the Convention and was the last to ratify.[i]

8. OUR BILL OF RIGHTS

Sources of the Bill of Rights

An early order of business in the First Congress was to propose a bill of rights to be submitted to the states for ratification. There were convenient models, because, as Edmund Randolph had noted, eight states had bills of rights, and there was Patrick Henry's from the Virginia ratification convention. In addition, there were the earlier precedents of John Locke from which they were drawn, especially his treatises concerning toleration and civil government. Educated men had read them.

From these sources they drafted the Bill of Rights, in ten articles. Many Americans are familiar with the First, which says, "Congress shall make no law respecting an establishment of religion, or prohibiting the free exercise thereof; or abridging the freedom of speech, or of the press; or the right of the people peaceably to assemble, and to petition the Government for a redress of grievances."

This derives from Locke's writings on toleration and from

Jefferson's "Virginia Statute for Religious Freedom." Jefferson believed that the nature of religion required that its freedom be recognized by law. The state should not oppose or support any particular religion, because the care of everyone's soul belongs to himself, and no one can prescribe the faith of another. Thus state religion was a contradiction in terms.

Religious liberty was not limited to any denomination, or even limited to Christians, but was extended without qualification. Jefferson regarded religious rights as "of the natural rights of mankind," which was Locke's concept. Locke's defense of religious freedom has become in part the classic defense not only of religious tolerance but also for freedom of expression in other matters, as enumerated in the First Amendment. Madison, following Locke, placed freedom of speech and religion among rights in property ("a man has a property in his rights").

Thomas Jefferson, disciple of Locke, wrote that it did him no injury if a man said he believed in one god or twenty. "It neither picks my pocket nor breaks my leg." This statement, ostensibly about religion, is one of his most telling ones about property — the man could hurt him by taking his property; whereas his religious opinions could not, illustrating yet again that rights in property are paramount. He believed in God, and while he was not a practicing Christian, he studied, admired, and wrote about the teachings of Jesus. Jefferson's opponents tried to make political capital out of the fact that he did not belong to a church and often called him an atheist — especially the New England clergy, who had strong ties to his opponents, the Federalist establishment.

It is government that could establish religion, or abridge freedom of speech or the press or the right of assembly under threat of Imprisonment (all of which it had done in the past). Therefore, the First Amendment was necessary, but while it contains very important rights, they are not the paramount "life, liberty and estates." This may seem a quibble, except that the US Supreme Court for seventy years has not given property rights the benefit of strict scrutiny it gives to First Amendment rights. To carry out the intent of the Framers, they must be equal.

The Second Amendment guarantees the right of the people to keep and bear arms. They saw national security as basic to protection of life, liberty and the pursuit of happiness, and provisions for an army, navy and militia had been included in Article I, Section 8 of the Constitution. Amendment Two was to guarantee the right to bear arms so citizens could defend themselves and bring their arms to militia service.

The Third Amendment provides the right not to have soldiers quartered in one's house without one's consent; that is a property right. Every man's home is his castle. The protection against unreasonable searches and seizures, Amendment Four, is similar.

The Heart of the Bill of Rights

Because the purpose of government is to protect property, including life, the heart of the Bill of Rights is in the Fifth Amendment, which specifies that one's life cannot be put in jeopardy except by indictment of a grand jury, nor can one for the same offense be twice put in jeopardy of life or limb (life and person are property), or be compelled to be a witness against oneself. No person may be "deprived of life, liberty, or property, without due process of law; nor shall private property be taken for public use, without just compensation." This is the key protection of rights under a government instituted to protect property.

Amendment Six guarantees the right of an accused to a speedy and public trial by an impartial jury, to be informed of the accusations, and to be confronted by the witnesses against him, and to have counsel for his defense. This is perhaps the ultimate defense against an abusive government. Jefferson thought that trial by jury was the only real anchor by which a government could be held to the principles of its constitution. As a corollary, there is a theory that a jury can release a prisoner if it believes that the law under which he is being tried is wrong, regardless of the judge's charge to the jury about the law in the case.

The Seventh Amendment also relates to the right of trial by jury in suits at common law. The Eighth prohibits excessive bail and cruel and unusual punishment — another protection for one's person and life. While some consider the death penalty to be cruel and unusual, "capital crimes" are mentioned in the Bill of Rights; it was the intent of the Founders to permit it.

Rights and Powers of the People and States

Amendments IX and X in recent years have not been accorded the respect they deserve. The Ninth states: "The enumeration in the Constitution, of certain rights, shall not be construed to deny or disparage others retained by the people." It is intended to give the Federal Government only those powers specifically assigned to it under the Constitution. It was the Framers' confidence in this principle that caused them to believe that a bill of rights was not necessary. They could not conceive that anyone might construe that it could do any more than they had allowed it. Fortunately, the people and their state governments insisted on a bill of rights, and they insisted that they retain all the rights not specifically delegated to the central government.

They drove home the point in Amendment Ten: "The powers not delegated to the United States by the Constitution, nor prohibited by it to the States, are reserved to the States respectively, or to the people."

In those final two articles of the Bill of Rights, the first Congress and the states made sure that the people were paramount. They had created a national government with carefully limited powers, leaving them in control of their rights to life, liberty and estates: their property. Those who like "flexibility" in constitutional interpretation tend to dismiss the Ninth and Tenth Amendments, but the Framers put them there as "clinchers" to limit the federal government.

9. JEFFERSON AND HAMILTON

The Beginning of the Rights Cycle

The turn of the 20th to the 21st century may seem a long way in time from the ratification of the Bill of Rights, but it is only two swings of the rights pendulum from it — swings that have tended to commence near the beginnings of centuries. The first began just before 1800, in Thomas Jefferson's muted campaign for the presidency, twelve years after the adoption of the Constitution. It was toward Lockean ideals.

Jefferson and Hamilton embodied the differences of opinion about the Constitution and shaped the debate that still goes on about government and the constitutional views of judges, so it is useful to examine the beliefs of the two men. In the election of 1800 the Republicans led by Thomas Jefferson routed the High Federalists of Alexander Hamilton. In that election Jefferson won the loyalty of the people with John Locke's ideas. Minimalist government triumphed over concentration of power; the states over the Federal Government. The people recaptured their rights.

The second swing in opinion came around 1900 — away from Jeffersonian rights. Some of the Progressives who led it sometimes called themselves "Hamiltonians." A third, if less definite, turn began about 1980 and may continue until similar results are achieved. In every poll people say they want less intrusion in their lives from the Federal government. In 1994, the Supreme Court made it clear that the people's rights in property were as important as their other rights, and in 1995 the Court reaffirmed the restraints on congressional powers of Article I, Section 8 of the Constitution. These rulings will be discussed at length.

In 1788 the new government of the United States began to function, though no precedents existed. George Washington was elected President, as everyone assumed he would be, and John Adams was elected Vice President, because he got the second-highest number of votes in the Electoral College. The President appointed Thomas Jefferson Secretary of State, an office which conducted foreign affairs and the few administrative functions of the government, except for the Treasury's responsibilities. Alexander Hamilton was Secretary of the Treasury.

The initial evolution of the role of the government was played out under the leadership of these two men, whose followers divided into political parties: Jefferson's Republicans and Hamilton's Federalists. The Republicans believed in the rule of the people under law and in a strictly-limited national government. The Federalists thought that the propertied elite should rule through a strong Federal government exercising wide powers.

Jefferson's Views

It may seem strange that Jefferson believed in Locke's ideal of protection of the individual's life, liberty and estates and yet did not think that holding property was a prerequisite of the right to vote, while Hamilton did. The distinction is that Jefferson wanted to open opportunities to the people to create wealth through their labor, while Hamilton's plan required that they have land and wealth to participate. Locke felt more strongly about a man's property in the "labour of his body and the work of his hands" than he did about money and real estate, so one could be a voter while he held only the potential for having property. Besides, he had a property in liberty and in his person under the Natural Law.

Hamilton's Mistrust of the People

Alexander Hamilton had a very different background than did Jefferson. He was born in the West Indies of a Scottish merchant father and a French Huguenot mother — and they were not married. He was a voracious reader of the classics and became a very good writer and a good businessman. Friends sent him to America for his education, which included Kings College, now Columbia University.

The American Revolution began when he was 13, and he became a pamphleteer and editorial writer by the age of 18. He used the press to attack politically and was in turn attacked. That he was familiar with history and the processes of government was evident in his writings. His sections of *The Federalist*, explaining the new Constitution, were brilliant. He did not agree with the

Convention but believed it important that its work be ratified.

He was always ambitious, so in the Revolution he wanted a command, but Washington made him an aide. It is a manifestation of his multiple interests that during the War he began to write about the need for a constitutional convention, and at the Annapolis Convention he argued so persuasively that the states agreed to call one.

He married into the aristocratic Schuyler family of New York, and he himself was an aristocrat by preference and temperament, cultivating the elite. He seldom made speeches to the masses, but rather to the leaders. His ideal government was the rule of "gentlemen," whom he thought were above striving for place, and he favored strong connections between government and men of wealth — a model realized in his national bank. He confessed to Washington that he "long since learned to hold public opinion of no value."[ii]

Hamilton's principal contribution to the Constitutional Convention was a five-hour speech in which he proposed election of a President and senators for life by electors with property. State governors were to have lifetime appointments from the president and the power of veto over state legislatures. State governments were to be effectively abolished. The President was to have the veto and to be able to enforce or ignore any law — he was to be an elective king. This proposal fell flat. It was not seconded or considered.

The last thing he said at the Convention was: "No man's ideas are more remote from the plan than my own are known to be; but is it possible to deliberate between anarchy and convulsion on one side, and the chance of good to be expected for the plan on the other?" Then he returned to New York, occasionally visiting the convention. At the conclusion, he was the only New York delegate present to sign, and he influenced the state's convention in its decision to ratify. Finally, he wrote influential passages for *The Federalist* in favor of ratification by the states.

His basic position never changed, and just before he retired from the Cabinet he declared himself a monarchist who had "no objections to a trial being made of this thing of a republic." Later he said that he had never had faith "from the beginning in a frail and worthless fabric." And yet, he was cited by the Supreme Court in 1936 as the authority on interpretation of the taxing and spending powers of Congress.

Limited vs. Powerful Government

Jefferson and Hamilton could hardly have been more different. Their theories foreshadowed the late 20th-century situation, with one group interested in limited national government empowering individuals and the other favoring direction of the economy by a powerful government wielding strong regulatory and taxing powers. The one trusts the people to make private contracts with each other to manage their affairs; the other does not.

Hamilton's actions indicated that he probably regarded himself as something akin to Prime Minister in Washington's cabinet. He tended to meddle in the affairs of other constitutional officers — certainly in Jefferson's Department of State. It caused friction between them, though Jefferson never complained publicly.

Hamilton worked out a plan for paying the public debt, including the excise taxes to do it. Jefferson had long since acknowledged that foreign debts must be paid, especially to France, which had financed the Revolution. Hamilton liked debt; Jefferson did not.

As to domestic debt, Hamilton repudiated the Continental currency and bills of credit, but he wanted to redeem certificates of indebtedness for loans, supplies, and services at face value, with interest. They had depreciated, and many of them had been bought by speculators at large discounts. They stood to make fortunes if the government redeemed them at face value. Hamilton was indifferent to these speculations. He also said that "a public debt is a public blessing," which foreshadowed later, more widespread, attitudes. Jefferson had a loathing for debt, personal or public.

Hamilton had a good point when he based assumption of state debts on the argument that they had been made in a common cause and that one plan was better than many. There was no legal obligation to assume them. Congressman James Madison, Jefferson's *protégé*, advocated against repudiation of Continental currency and bills and against payment to current holders of debt at the market rate, with the balance to go to the original holders, many of whom had been soldiers in the Revolution. The soldiers, he said, would lose 7/8ths of their money, while the speculators would gain by 7 or 8 times.

Madison's plan was voted down, and it was later determined that 29 out of the 64 members of the House were holders of securities (Hamilton was never accused of chicanery). It was a strategic victory for Jefferson, however, because the people were awakened to the fact that the wealthy were enriching themselves at their expense. As noted earlier, the Northern states were the most in arrears in payment of their debts, so Southerners would be taxed to pay Northern debt and speculators. The war of words and the lobbying were fierce, and there were rumors of vote buying by the Hamiltonians. They lost by two votes, but Hamilton was still determined to win.

A Political Deal

Another question difficult to resolve politically was where to locate the Federal District: New York, Philadelphia, Baltimore, along the Susquehanna River or the Delaware, at Georgetown, or elsewhere on the Potomac. It was of no matter to Hamilton, but he knew that it was to Jefferson and the Southerners. Backstage negotiations were conducted for votes. Jefferson let it be known that a deal could be made: assumption of the debt in exchange for location of the Federal city on the banks of the Potomac. Credit to the states for payments they had made on the debt was included in the deal as an enticement in particular to Virginia, which had paid off most of its debt.

Congress voted Hamilton his debt assumption.

Hamilton's National Bank

His next, and most famous, policy venture was creation of a national bank, a monopoly of banking; again, something the merchants and monied people wanted. First, he delivered a report in support of it, which included a review of the history of banking and the banking experience of other nations. It was not to be a reserve bank, like today's Federal Reserve; it would be a commercial bank. The proposal passed the Senate easily, but when it got to the House, Madison, "the Father of the Constitution," spoke against it, pointing out that it was not authorized. Hamilton conceded that it was not, but invoked the doctrine of "implied powers." Madison countered that an endless chain of such powers could be foreseen unless Congress stayed close to the letter of the supreme law. (John C. Calhoun in 1837 argued against an appropriation to buy Madison's notes on the Constitutional Convention on the grounds that such a purchase was not specifically authorized by the Constitution. Madison probably would have agreed).

The House joined the Senate in giving Hamilton his national bank.

General Welfare Clause

Jefferson had opposed the bank and had given his opinion when George Washington requested it. He advocated "strict construction" of the Constitution and contended that its words meant precisely what they said. He thought the "General Welfare" clause was a statement of the purpose for which the specific power of laying taxes was to be exercised, not a grant to Congress of a distinct and independent power to do anything it pleased if it thought it was good for the Union. Such an interpretation "would reduce the whole instrument to a single phrase." Locke had said that everyone must pay his share for the protection of government, which was the principle of the General Welfare clause, and the taxes and expenditures were only to be for government's property-protection functions. Concerning the "necessary and proper" clause ("To make all laws which shall be necessary and proper for carrying into Execution the foregoing Powers, and all other Powers vested by this Constitution . . ."), Jefferson denied that those means that were merely "convenient" could be regarded as "necessary." Such latitude would "swallow up all the delegated powers." Hamilton took his opposition personally.

These opposing views of how to interpret the Constitution are today at the center of discussion in the United States. "Flexible" judicial constructions have reduced the Constitution to a single welfare phrase and have swallowed up the delegated powers. Jefferson foresaw what was to happen in the Progressive and New Deal eras.

Alien and Sedition Laws

The principal political issues of the day concerned America's attitude toward the French Revolution: Jefferson tended to be in sympathy with France, Hamilton with its enemy, Britain. The Federalists passed Alien and Sedition Laws to suppress the Republicans. After Congress adjourned in 1798, Jefferson convened a conference at Monticello to launch a protest movement against the Alien and Sedition Laws through resolutions of the legislatures of the states, pronouncing the Laws in violation of the Constitution and void. Jefferson secretly drafted those of Kentucky, while Madison drafted Virginia's. In Congress, Republican attempts to speak on the subject were repressed.

The battle for supremacy in the election of 1800 began, with the Alien and Sedition laws at issue. The fever for war with France subsided as the cost was realized. The war taxes aroused bitter resentment. A vote on a declaration of war against France was forced by the Federalists in Congress against President Adams' wishes, but he prevailed by a small margin. Hamilton had lost control of his Party.

His loss was confirmed when Adams sent new emissaries to France, having been assured that they would be received. There would be no war for a General Hamilton to lead. The Jeffersonians were jubilant. Adams had won against his own party. He knew that he would be a one-term president, but he wrote later that he asked no better epitaph than the recognition that he had taken upon himself the responsibility of maintaining the peace with France.

The Federalists knew they were in trouble in the upcoming presidential election, and they hatched a law to rob Jefferson of the office through an electoral committee that would operate in secret. The plan was leaked to the newspapers, and died. Jefferson shaped his party's platform: oppose the Alien and Sedition laws, the direct tax, the large army and navy, "the usurious loan these follies set on foot." The Government should be rigorously frugal. Savings should be applied to the public debt. Have political connections with no nation. Preserve the liberty of speech and the freedom of the press.

Jefferson Victorious

Hamilton could not reconcile himself with President John Adams, who was proving much too independent, having finally fired the disloyal Cabinet officers he had inherited from George Washington. The former Treasury Secretary plotted to divide the Federalist electoral vote, so that Adams could not win. General Pinckney of South Carolina was his choice.

A scandal was discovered. Speaker Dayton had requisitioned much more money than was needed to compensate the House and was found to have kept much of it himself. Federalist difficulties were compounded when John Adams said that he did not believe that the United States could exist as a nation unless the Executive was hereditary. Noah Webster, of his party, said that the poorer classes should be excluded from the vote. A Federalist editor denounced "the stupid populace, too abject in ignorance to think rightly, and too depraved to draw honest deductions." There was hint of secession of the New England states in the event of Jefferson's election, though the Republicans were actually making gains there.

Electoral intrigues intensified. There was a movement among Federalists to elect Aaron Burr, and Hamilton declared that he would rather have Jefferson as President. The Virginian was certainly the choice of the people.

The election was held in the House, by states, the Electoral College having tied. On the first ballot Jefferson won eight states, with nine needed for election. Votes were taken all through the day and night. The twenty-eighth vote was at noon the next day, and there was more balloting over the following days.

It was evident that the public was for Jefferson. Finally, a Vermont Federalist elector withdrew, allowing his state's other elector to vote for Jefferson, and the Maryland Federalists cast blank ballots. Delaware's delegate also cast a blank one, and Jefferson was elected.

The Federalists had one more card to play: the "midnight appointment" of many judges and magistrates, confirmed hurriedly by the strongly Federalist Senate. One of the appointments was given to a Mr. Marbury, subject of the **Marbury v. Madison** case that established the Supreme Court's authority to review acts of Congress. Another was John Marshall as Chief Justice, who as Secretary of State had signed Marbury's and the other commissions and who carried Federalist principles to the bench for many more years.

At noon, Thomas Jefferson walked from his boarding house to the Capitol and made a healing speech. Chief Justice Marshall administered the oath of office.

Jefferson was President. The ideals of John Locke had resonated with the people and were destined to guide American government for a hundred years.

10. Jefferson's Minimalist Government

Jefferson's Program

President Thomas Jefferson repealed taxes, provided for retirement of the public debt, fought the Barbary pirates who were harassing American shipping in the Mediterranean, and bought the Louisiana Territory from France. There is evidence that he struggled with the constitutionality of the Louisiana Purchase, because the treaty of 1783 had established the limits of the United States. To a friend he made the argument that: "Our peculiar security is in the possession of a written Constitution. Let us not make it a blank paper by construction."[iii] Yet he explained that: "A strict observance of the written laws is doubtless one of the high duties of a good citizen, but it is not the highest. The laws of necessity, of self-preservation, of saving our country by a scrupulous adherence to written law, would be to lose the law itself, with life, liberty, property and all those who are enjoying them with us; thus absurdly sacrificing the end to the means . . ." without a specific grant of power to do so in the Constitution. This is the police power — Locke's "executive power of the people" — employed on a grand scale. Jefferson evidently believed that by owning the Purchase land his government was providing protection for its existing territory and for the people from France, Spain and England who lived in the new lands. The states brought into the Union from the Louisiana Territory were entitled to the same rights as the original ones, thanks to the Constitution and the precedent Jefferson had established in the Kentucky Resolutions and in the Virginia Constitution, which was emulated by other states and in the United States Constitution.

His response to Britain's imperious trade policies and impressment of American seamen into service on its ships was a trade embargo. It nearly caused the New England states with their strong commercial and shipping interests to secede. His policy was proved practical, because war was avoided at a time when the nation was weak.

Strict Construction

Jefferson governed in minimalist style, performing only the functions specifically delegated by the people and the states in the Constitution. He construed it very strictly, because he knew its spirit from his "immortal" guide, John Locke, and its letter because James Madison, the "Father of the Constitution," was his Secretary of State and confidant.

Jefferson was always concerned that the General Welfare clause of the Constitution might be misused as authority to spend on unauthorized objects. The General Welfare was promoted by the functions of government that protected property rights, and the delegates gave the federal government only the powers that would fulfill that function.

Stephen Moore of the Cato Institute has provided statements of Founders and others on the subject. In 1798 Jefferson wrote, "Congress has not unlimited powers to provide for the General Welfare, but only those specifically enumerated." Madison had written in 1794 about a $15,000 appropriation for French refugees: "I cannot undertake to lay my finger on that article of the Constitution which granted a right to Congress of expending on objects of benevolence, the money of their constituents." Madison added that any unwarranted government interference, no matter how righteous or well intended, would be "but the first link of a long chain of repetitions;"[iv] this from the man who attended all the sessions of the constitutional convention and took the detailed, authoritative notes on it. He was certainly prescient about the repetitions.

Daniel Webster later argued that Congress has the powers to make all Laws that shall be necessary and proper for carrying into execution its other powers. "Let the end be legitimate, let it be within the scope of the Constitution, and all means which are appropriate, which are plainly adapted to that end, which are not prohibited, but consist with the letter and spirit of the Constitution, are constitutional."[v] This paralleled Chief Justice John Marshall's views and Hamilton's doctrine of "implied powers." This was expanded over succeeding years to allow Congress to do almost anything it wished in taxing and spending. Even Webster's definition does not justify the welfare state, because Congress's "other powers" are still only those enumerated to protect property, which is the "legitimate end" and "within the scope of the Constitution."

The General Welfare argument continued. In 1827, the year after Jefferson's death, Colonel Davy Crockett was elected to Congress. During his first session a bill was offered for the relief of a widow of a naval officer. Said Crockett on the House floor: "We must not permit our respect for the dead or our sympathy for the living to lead us into an act of injustice to the balance of the living. I will not attempt to prove that Congress has no power to appropriate this money as an act of charity. Every member upon this floor knows it. We have the right as individuals, to give away as much of our own money as we please in charity; but as members of Congress we have no right to appropriate a dollar of the public money." It had been assumed that the bill would pass easily, but it failed, getting only a few affirmative votes. And it is said that Crockett, one of the poorer members of Congress, was the only one to contribute substantially to a private charity fund for the widow.

The Federalists argued that the General Welfare clause gave Congress a generalized spending authority. In response South Carolina Senator William Drayton asked, "Can it be conceived that the great and wise men who devised our Constitution should have failed so egregiously as to grant a power which rendered restriction upon power practically unavailing? If Congress can determine what constitutes the General Welfare and can appropriate money for its advancement, where is the limitation to carrying into execution whatever can be effected by money." He had reached the heart of the matter.

Social reformer Dorothea Dix led the fight for a bill in 1854 to help the mentally ill. President Franklin Pierce vetoed it and was castigated; but, said he, "I cannot find any authority in the Constitution for public charity. To approve such spending would be contrary to the letter and the spirit of the Constitution and subversive to the whole theory upon which the Union of these States is founded."

Grover Cleveland vetoed hundreds of spending bills sent to him by Congress in the late 1800s because he could "find no warrant for such an appropriation in the Constitution."[ii] The government's main expenditures in the 19th century were for the military, a property-protection function. The principal departure came with the New Deal; the first, though, came with the federal income tax in 1913. It was a popular idea at the time, because it only affected the very highest incomes and most people did not expect to pay it. Only two percent had to file at all.

Supreme Court Established as Interpreter

The **Marbury v. Madison** decision by the Supreme Court under Federalist Chief Justice John Marshall had established in 1803 the Court's authority to review and overturn laws of Congress, but the opinion was viewed during Jefferson's presidency not as a judicial precedent but simply as a political setback. Secretary of State Madison had to deliver Marbury's justice of the peace commission under a writ of *mandamus*.

It shows that jurisprudence can be more influential than politics. In 1798, during the Adams Administration, the Supreme Court's **Calder v. Bull** decision said that: "There are acts which the Federal, or State, Legislature cannot do without exceeding their authority . . . An act . . . contrary to the great first principles of the social compact, cannot be considered a rightful exercise of legislative authority." Justice Chase was not relying on the words of the Constitution only, but rather on the Natural Law from which it sprang. If it was in conflict, it was wrong on the face of it, because that was what the system was all about. Justice Iredell preferred to rely on the specific delegations of power, but he believed that laws must stay strictly within those powers. In **Fletcher v. Peck** in 1810 Chief Justice Marshall thought that a Georgia law invalidating a land grant could be struck down "either by general principles which are common to our free institutions, or by the particular provisions of the constitution of the United States."

There were several Supreme Court cases that established principles of law in the decades immediately following Jefferson's presidency. The **Dartmouth College** case in 1819 asserted that the federal government could enforce the sanctity of contracts, a decision upholding Locke's principle that private contracts are the paramount instrument of society. In that same year Marshall's Court held, in **M'Culloch v. Maryland**, that the State of Maryland could not tax the Bank of the United States — setting aside a state law on constitutional grounds. Then in 1824 in **Gibbons vs. Ogden** the Court asserted Federal control over interstate commerce. Gradually, the interstate commerce doctrine was expanded to the extent that in 1942 the Supreme Court held that a farmer was not allowed to plant 23 acres of wheat instead of the 11 allotted him by the Government and keep the 239 bushels from the extra acreage for his own use, because it *affected* interstate commerce, even though it would not move in it. In **Gibbons,** the Court cited Marshall's statement that the Commerce Clause restraints must be political rather than judicial. The Court therefore allowed Congress to do almost anything it wanted to in the regulation of commerce.

Sometimes it is not evident when a "can of worms" is being opened, and the Court's statement in **Gibbons** is an example.

These cases had more to do with the organization and the powers of the Federal Government and the states than they did with civil rights. While they went further in the direction of national supremacy than Jefferson would have liked, they were not tests of Lockean rights. The main period of legislation and adjudication on individual rights came early in the 20th century.

Civil War Fought for Lockean Principle

In the meantime, there was civil war — only 53 years from the end of Jefferson's presidency. It was fought to preserve the principles of the Declaration of Independence and the political union based upon them. Slavery was one of the issues. Jefferson opposed slavery, because it was completely at variance with his ideas of liberty. His view was shared by many of the Founders.

Compromises were made, such as pairing the admission to the Union of free and slave states, but the issue festered in the body politic. It was impossible for a nation that professed individual freedom as its bedrock value to live the lie that some of its people were not entitled to be free.

The system of Lockean rights had to be extended to all of the humans in the nation. Some Southern states did not want to secede: North Carolina probably would not have done so, had it not been bracketed between South Carolina and Virginia; its piedmont and western farmers had few or no slaves, and the state opposed secession until Lincoln called for troops to fight the South. The western part of Virginia, composed of non-slave-holding mountaineers, broke away, became West Virginia, and remained with the Union.

The Civil War was certainly one of the major turns toward the philosophy of John Locke, and he was invoked indirectly. President Lincoln drew on his spirit when he based his policy on the Declaration of Independence. Locke was against slavery; his ideas were the official beliefs of America, and it was living a lie. The issue was resolved by a terrible war, instead of by an election or court ruling.

Rights At the End of the 19th Century

Rights in property had been protected since the founding of our Nation, as we have seen, and it is especially instructive to examine their treatment from 1887 to 1936, before their being downgraded by the New Deal-era justices. Before and during that period capital and the work force were expanding rapidly, and many workers were by then in factories, rather than on farms. Issues concerning working conditions, wages and hours began to come before the Supreme Court. This fifty-year period has been termed one of "substantive due process" in the courts. The term refers to the provision of the Fifth Amendment to the Constitution, which says: "No person shall . . . be deprived of life, liberty, or property, without due process of law." It was almost a quotation from Locke's *Second Treatise of Government.* During this time the Court enforced the substance of the Fifth Amendment.

Beginning of the Era

The era of substantive due process was initiated by **Mugler v. Kansas** in 1887, which sustained a law prohibiting intoxicating beverages. In this case, the Court announced that it was prepared to examine the substantive reasonableness of state legislation, saying that not "every statute enacted ostensibly for the promotion of the public morals, the public health, or the public safety would be accepted as a legitimate exertion of the police powers of the State." The courts could not be "misled by mere pretenses"; rather, they were obligated "to look at the substance of things." Accordingly, if a purported exercise of the police power "has no real or substantial relation to those objects, or is a palpable invasion of rights secured by the fundamental law, it is the duty of the courts to so adjudge." This era, in which rights in property were strictly upheld, is sometimes referred to as **"Allgeyer-Adair-Coppage-Lochner"** (Allgeyer v. Louisiana, 1897; **Lochner v. New York,** 1905; **Adair v. United States,** 1908; **Coppage v. Kansas,** 1915).

The substantive due process decisions were severely criticized by some later Supreme Court justices and others, who felt that the justices of that period were attempting to enshrine *laissez faire* ("let it be") economic policy. If some justices were doing that, and to the extent that they were, it was no more principled than the New Deal Court's later social engineering. However, the statement above from **Mugler v. Kansas** about examination of a purported exercise of the police power to determine if it "is a palpable invasion of rights secured by fundamental law" indicates that they were trying to hold to principle and were not simply enshrining *laissez faire*. A better constitutional approach might have been to protect labor by enforcing its property rights, which in Locke's view were extremely important: "of the products of the earth useful to the life of man, nine-tenths are the effect of labor." The man without land had a property in his labor, and it was the most important property. He was as rich in rights as a country gentleman.

Ever since Jefferson, the courts had tended to uphold property rights strictly, which was not controversial at all until the Industrial Revolution, a stage of economic growth in which large amounts of capital and big enterprises employing huge numbers of workers were necessary to produce and process large quantities of raw materials, to build the industrial infrastructure (such as railroads and shipping). Some businesses took advantage of their power over individuals who had little of it. Because of the large industrial organizations that were being formed, and the crowding into cities that resulted, reformers began to advocate social regulation.

In **Allgeyer v. Louisiana** (1897), the Court ruled that the state could not make it illegal to buy marine insurance from a company not licensed in the state. It relied on the due process clause and ruled that the state statute violated the Fourteenth Amendment (which forbade the states from abridging the privileges and immunities of citizens of the United States and extended the due process clause to the states) by depriving the Allgeyer firm of its right to unrestrained contract for insurance. Justice Peckham, writing for a unanimous Court, declared: "The liberty mentioned in that amendment means not only the right of the citizen to be free from the mere physical restraint of his person, as by incarceration, but the term is deemed to embrace the right of the citizen to be free in the enjoyment of all his faculties; to be free to use them in all lawful ways; to live and work where he will; to earn his livelihood by any lawful calling; to pursue any livelihood or avocation, and for that purpose to enter into all contracts which may be proper, necessary and essential to his carrying out to a successful conclusion the purposes above mentioned" (to earn a living).

Property Rights Setback

The 19th century was not a completely smooth road for property rights. In 1872 the US Supreme Court had dealt them a setback, ruling that Louisiana could set up a monopoly of the slaughterhouse business in several of its parishes, though the monopoly had damaged the businesses of others. Justice Bradley's minority opinion in the second **Slaughter-House** case stated: "The right to follow any of the common occupations of life is an inalienable right. It was formulated as such under the 'phrase pursuit of happiness' in the Declaration of Independence, which commenced with the fundamental proposition that 'all men are created equal, that they are endowed by their Creator with certain inalienable rights; that among these are life, liberty and the pursuit of happiness'. This right is a large ingredient in the civil liberty of the citizen . . . I hold that liberty of pursuit — the right to follow any of the ordinary callings of life — is one of the privileges of a citizen in the United States."

In that particular case, however, a majority of the Court was not prepared to regard a person's calling or labor as property. They could have checked the *Second Treatise of Government*" which was, through the Common Law, the source of the property rights they were interpreting. To Locke it was a very important element of property, and the men who wrote the Constitution were installing his doctrine.

Twenty-five years after **Slaughter-House**, in his **Allgeyer** opinion Justice Peckham also cited an opinion by the first Justice Harlan: "The main proposition advanced by the defendant is that his enjoyment upon terms of equality with all others in similar circumstances of the privilege of pursuing an ordinary calling or trade, and of acquiring, holding and selling property, is an essential part of his rights of liberty and property, as guaranteed by the Fourteenth Amendment. The court assents to this general proposition as embodying a sound principle of constitutional law."

Right to Make a Living Is Fundamental

These judges were saying that a person has a right to make a living, and to make choices and contracts for it, uninhibited by government permits or licenses. Bradley and Harlan built their opinions on the seamless rock of our liberties: the Declaration of Independence, the Bill of Rights, the Common Law, and Locke. Forty years later the Court shifted to the sands of "rational relation to a public purpose" and to "penumbras from emanations from the Constitution;" *i.e.*, whatever nine men (often a majority of five) wanted to rule, to uphold the social theories of the day.

In 1895 New York enacted a 60-hour work week for bakeries, with a maximum of ten hours per day. A Mr. Lochner, bakery owner, had been indicted for violating this provision and convicted by the trial court, which ruling was upheld by appellate courts. He said that the law violated his liberty under the due process clause. The state argued that the law was designed to protect the health of workers and was, therefore, a legitimate use of the police power to protect health and safety.

In the 1905 **Lochner v. New York** ruling, the Court said: "The act must have a . . . direct relation, as a means to an end, and the end itself must be appropriate and legitimate, before an act can be held to be valid which interferes with the general right of an individual to be free in his person and in his power to contract in relation to his own labor." The right to contract between employer and employee is protected by the due process clauses unless special circumstances overcome that strong presumption. "There must be more than the mere fact of the possible existence of some small amount of unhealthiness to warrant legislative interference with liberty."

In recent years this doctrine has been upended. The slightest suspicion of unhealthiness has sometimes generated strict regulations, as in the banning of the Alar preservative for apples (later shown to be scientifically unjustified) and of substances that can cause cancer in rats that have been stuffed with them. This kind of regulation has been sustained by the modern courts.

A lesson from **Lochner** is that legislatures tend to control livelihoods and to determine the conditions under which citizens will be allowed to pursue "happiness." Said the Supreme Court in **Lochner**: "It might be safely affirmed that almost all occupations more or less affect the health . . . It is unfortunately true that labor, even in any department, may possibly carry with it the seeds of unhealthiness. But are we all, on that account, at the mercy of legislative majorities? A printer, a tinsmith, a locksmith, a carpenter, a cabinetmaker, a dry good clerk, a bank's, a lawyer's, or a physician's clerk, or a clerk in almost any kind of business, would all come under the power of the legislature, on this assumption. No trade, no occupation, no mode of earning one's living could escape this all-pervading power, and the acts of the legislature in limiting the hours of labor in all employments would be valid, although such limitation might seriously cripple the ability of the laborer to support himself and his family . . .

"It is also urged, pursuing the same line of argument, that it is to the interest of the State that its population should be strong and robust, and therefore any legislation which may be said to tend to make people healthy must be valid as health laws, enacted under the police power. If this be a valid argument and a justification for this kind of legislation, it follows that the protection of the Federal Constitution from undue interference with liberty of person and freedom of contract is visionary, wherever the law is sought to be justified as a valid exercise of the police power. Scarcely any law but might find shelter under such assumptions, and conduct, property so called, as well as contract, would come under the restrictive sway of the legislature."

Justice Holmes, Dissenter

In dissent, Justice Oliver Wendell Holmes said: "This case is decided upon an economic theory which a large part of the country does not entertain. If it were a question whether I agreed with that theory, I should desire to study it further and long before making up my mind. But I do not conceive that to be my duty, because I strongly believe that my agreement or disagreement has nothing to do with the right of a majority to embody their opinions in law. It is settled by various decisions of this court that (state laws) may regulate life in many ways which we as legislators might think as injudicious or if you like as tyrannical as this, and which equally with this interfere with the liberty to contract . . . The liberty of the citizen to do as he likes so long as he does not interfere with the liberty of others to do the same, which has been a shibboleth for some well-known writers, is interfered with by school laws, by the Post Office, by every state or municipal institution which takes his money for purposes thought desirable, whether he likes it or not. The 14th Amendment does not enact Mr. Herbert Spencer's Social Statics . . . a constitution is not intended to embody a particular economic theory, whether of paternalism and the organic relation of the citizen to the State or of *laissez faire*. It is made for people of fundamentally differing views, and the accident of our finding certain opinions natural and familiar or novel and even shocking ought not to conclude our judgment upon the question whether statutes embodying them conflict with the (Constitution).

" . . . I think that the word liberty in the 14th Amendment is perverted when it is held to prevent the natural outcome of a dominant opinion, unless it can be said that a rational and fair man necessarily would admit that the statute proposed would infringe fundamental principles as they have been understood by the traditions of our people and our law . . ."

Why did he invent the "rational and fair man" as the arbiter, instead of affirming that judges must follow the fundamental principles of the Constitution? He took the political route, advocating "the right of a majority to embody their opinions in law," though we have a Constitution to prevent the passage of certain kinds of laws by the majority — those which transgress rights in property. It is what is meant by "government of laws and not of men."

All of the tradition of Lockean law argues that the Constitution exists to protect against "the natural outcome of dominant opinion"; against the possible tyranny of the majority.

Holmes' statement that laws are often used to regulate injudiciously, and that liberty is often interfered with, is used to justify more of the same — rather than seeking to limit the abuses using the words and intent of the Bill of Rights.

Justice Holmes evidently thought that the Court's majority was trying to uphold *laissez faire*, the "economic theory that a large part of the country does not entertain." He follows this with his reference to "Mr. Herbert Spencer's *Social Statics*." Spencer, an Englishman, lived from 1820 to 1903. He was passionate for human freedom — a libertarian and believer in *laissez faire* economics. The leading sociologist of 19th century England, he wrote *The Man Versus the State*, *Principles of Sociology* and other influential treatises, and he had a great impact on social and economic thinking in the United States as well as in England.

Holmes did not prevail in **Lochner**. He dissented, as he often did. The Court's majority in that and other cases of the time required legislatures to show compelling reasons for regulating people's lives. More recently, the courts will discover a plausible "reason" even if the lawmakers have none, as law professor Bernard Siegan points out: in the modern era the Court has held that only " . . . the invidious discrimination, the wholly arbitrary act" violated the Fourteenth Amendment (**City of New Orleans v. Dukes**, 1976). It has been observed by a Supreme Court justice that any law that legislators pass will be sustained unless they were in a complete state of lunacy at the time they acted.[iii]

Labor Protected by Contracts

Adair v. United States (1907) and **Coppage v. Kansas** (1915) involved what the unions called "yellow dog" contracts, in which workers had contracted not to join a union and were therefore fired when they engaged in union activities. The question was whether the legislature could pass a law outlawing these contracts. Proponents of the law said that unions were essential for the public welfare. Justice Harlan wrote, in **Adair**: "The right of a person to sell his labor upon such terms as he deems proper is, in its essence, the same as the right of the purchaser of labor to prescribe the conditions upon which he will accept such labor from the person offering to sell it. So the right of the employee to quit the service of the employer, for whatever reason, is the same as the right of the employer, for whatever reason, to dispense with the service of such employee."

The question above about whether unions are essential for the public welfare is worthy of thoughtful consideration by conservatives. Locke believed that one's labor was his property — the most important element of property. He also believed in the right to make contracts, and unions are contracts between workers to bargain jointly, giving them more strength than they would have separately. The unions, in turn, may make contracts with employers. This is the way to protect the workers, rather than by government regulations that restrict the right of contract, such as family leave and minimum wage laws. A worker should be able to bargain for higher wages, more benefits, or anything else, which she may not be able to do if the company has to spend its money on replacements for her or lose her work output when she takes the weeks of maternity leave that the employer must allow her by government mandate.

The question, then, is whether workers do or do not have the freedom to contract for membership to protect their own welfare. The public welfare is always protected by freedom of contract, unless the contract damages someone else — in which case it can be curbed by lawsuit or the "police power" of government (from *polis*, the Greek word for state or citizenship), traditionally understood to be necessary to protect public health and safety. Locke called it the "executive power" of people to protect their rights.

Justice Pitney said, in **Coppage,** that the employer requirement of not joining a union was no worse than one that the employee work full time for only one employer, and that whenever the right of private property exists, "there must and will be inequalities of fortune; and thus it naturally happens that parties negotiating about a contract are not equally unhampered by circumstances. . . . This applies to all contracts, and not merely to that between employer and employee. Indeed a little reflection will show that wherever the right of private property and the right of free contract coexist, each party when contracting is inevitably more or less influenced by the question whether he has much property, or little, or none; for the contract is made to the very end that each may gain something that he needs or desires more urgently than that which he proposes to give in exchange. And, since it is self-evident that, unless all things are held in common, some persons must have more property than others, it is from the nature of things impossible to uphold freedom of contract and the right of private property without at the same time recognizing as legitimate those inequalities of fortune that are the necessary result of the exercise of those rights."

In noting that in freely-made contracts "each may gain something that he needs or desires more urgently than that which he proposes to give in exchange," Justice Pitney put his finger on the condition for economic growth: both parties gain in a freely-made contract. On the other hand, when government limits the right to contract — as in zoning, where the buyer may not be able put land to its highest and best use; or where it mandates a minimum wage, so that a job worth less than that wage is not even offered to an unskilled worker — one or the other party does not gain, and there is no growth. With economic growth more people are able to provide for themselves, and less welfare spending and intervention are needed, with their attendant regulations that further inhibit contracts. The limiting of Lockean rights has been extremely damaging to the individuals who make up the economy of the United States, and especially to the poor, who need all possible opportunities opened to them.

Judges who had received their education or started their law practice during the Civil War era espoused freedom of contract very strongly, because it was believed that the right of the individual to work for whom and how he pleased was among the rights for which the Civil War had been fought. That war was a violent turn toward Lockean rights, made necessary because the human rights of the slaves had not been protected by government. There is no freedom of contract in slavery. President Lincoln employed Jefferson and the Declaration as the ideological "big guns" in the War.

Substantive Due Process Said to Be "Discredited"

Justice Hugo Black in the 1930s called the **Lochner**, **Adair** and **Coppage** rulings "discredited." He may have believed that the Court was trying to impose a *laissez-faire* economic policy. He had been a senator who supported New Deal legislation, so he stood with the group that wanted strong curbs on private enterprise. He was on the Court in the period in which laws were upheld that had only a rational relation to a public purpose, and in which the burden of proof was on the individual to show why the legislature could not pass a law that restricted his rights.

The **Lochner**, **Adair** and **Coppage** cases upheld economic rights even where working-condition, health and union issues were allegedly involved, because the states did not make compelling cases for their necessity. The Court was properly putting the burden of proof on government. It stated that it was not intruding on the legislature's functions but was enforcing constitutionally guaranteed rights. The Constitution limited the power of government to diminish the right of contract and gave constitutional status to liberty of contract.[VIII] This is the correct interpretation, considering that the Lockean system is one of freedom of contract between individuals, and that our government is based on a contract with the people.

The period of "substantive due process" was one in which property rights were generally upheld. It was followed by the Progressive and the New Deal eras, in which they often were not.

12. THE PROGRESSIVES

Rights in the 20th Century

The cycle of attitude toward rights in American politics and jurisprudence has been traced as far as the end of the 19th century, with Locke's and Jefferson's doctrine substantially intact, despite some regulatory intervention by the Progressives such as the creation of the Interstate Commerce Commission. The dramatic changes came in the 20th.

The public's view of rights and the role of government changed as the Industrial Revolution progressed. Industry brought people into the cities and into work in which they were no longer individual entrepreneurs such as farmers, even sharecroppers, had been. Long hours were viewed as the way to "get ahead," but workers were increasingly regimented and often labored in unhealthful, dangerous conditions, and children were sometimes pressed into adult work.

As noted earlier, it was an era of big enterprises, in which some of the business leaders became very rich. It is sometimes ridiculed as "the era of the robber barons," though the barons employed large labor forces and so supported families, and they donated libraries and opera houses and endowed universities. The pursuit of self-interest is a Lockean concept, and self interest leads people to make money for their families foremost, to be philanthropic at times, and to be greedy occasionally.

The Progressives

The reaction against abuses by industry brought on the "Progressive Movement" with Theodore Roosevelt's inauguration in 1902. It was the beginning of a swing away from Lockean rights. The cycle of attitudes toward property rights was on the hundred-year schedule. He (and Taft and Wilson, after him) saw themselves as "liberal conservatives" who accepted the new industrial order but wanted to regulate it. Elihu Root, cabinet member in the McKinley and Theodore Roosevelt Administrations, said that industrial development demanded the "readjustment of the relations between great bodies of men and the establishment of new legal rights and obligations not contemplated when existing laws were passed or existing limitations upon the powers of government were prescribed in our Constitution. . . ." He noted the complicated relationships between the many groups in business and society, "for the solution of which the old reliance upon the free action of individual wills appears quite inadequate. And in many directions the intervention of that organized control which we call government seems necessary to produce the same result of justice and right conduct which obtained through the attrition of individuals before the new conditions arose."[xx]

Some new laws were needed, but the old Constitutional guarantees of property and limitations on the powers of government were still valid. It is never right for our government to take away protection of life, liberty and the pursuit of happiness, because that is the reason for its existence. He and like-minded leaders should have proposed amendments to the Constitution for "the establishment of new legal rights and obligations," instead of trying to bend the Constitution to fit their objectives. However, that was only a prelude to the "torturing" to come.

Root and other Progressives were, they felt sure, able to use the power of government to do good; no more "free action of individual wills"; no more Lockean freedom to make contracts. The action of principled bureaucrats would replace the effect of politicians. What they did not sufficiently take into account was that, while the money interests were powerful, government is more powerful; it has the power of capital punishment and all lesser penalties, which Locke reckoned to be the real power. Although industry was big, the restraint could have been applied by enforcing labor's property rights and through Lockean contractual institutions: unions and collective bargaining. Organizations sprang up to advocate, for example, against child labor abuses, and they had considerable effect through the power of information and education.

Theodore Roosevelt noted that the Progressives were in two camps: one represented "a kind of rural Toryism, which wishes to attempt the impossible task of returning to the economic conditions that obtained sixty years ago . . . to bust the trusts into competing units . . . . The other half wishes to recognize the inevitableness of combinations in business, and meet it by a corresponding increase in governmental power over big business."

The wing represented by William Jennings Bryan and Louis Brandeis were more afraid of big government than of big money. The other wing, whose ideology was spearheaded by Herbert Croley, founder of *The New Republic* magazine, wanted a "welfare state" controlled by Congress and staffed by intelligent and dedicated bureaucrats. The President chose this way, abetted by allies including Judge Learned Hand and Supreme Court justice-to-be Felix Frankfurter, among others. They considered themselves Federalists, followers of the tradition of Hamilton.

Theodore Roosevelt called the 25 years before his Administration: "A riot of individualistic materialism, under which complete freedom for the individual . . . turned out in practice to mean perfect freedom for the strong to wrong the weak . . ." He turned to strong regulation, the only "proper" course in his mind.

The Progressive alternative to regulation, as explained above, was trust busting. One of Locke's beliefs was that monopoly was wrong: he said that enough must be left for everyone. In truly free markets, it is difficult to maintain a monopoly because there is an opportunity to compete (especially true now, in the "idea" economy of high technology). Besides, in its next phase, industry evolved in general into smaller units, and in our present day mostly to very small ones — a situation which does not require the same sort of regulation, even if it were constitutional. Roosevelt, Croley, Hand, Frankfurter and the other Progressives abandoned Locke, Jefferson and the Constitution to start the welfare state.

The World Adopts, We Abandon

Friedrich Hayek makes an interesting observation on this change of political philosophy in America from restricted government to democratic socialism. "A large part of the people of the world borrowed from Western civilization and adopted Western ideals at a time when the West had become unsure of itself and had largely lost faith in the traditions that have made it what it is. This was at a time when the intellectuals of the West had to a great extent abandoned the very belief in freedom which, by enabling the West to make full use of those forces that are responsible for the growth of all civilization, had made its unprecedented quick growth possible. In consequence, those men from the less advanced nations who became purveyors of ideas to their own people learned, during their Western training, not how the West had built up its civilization, but mostly those dreams of alternatives which its very success had engendered."[x]

13. FROM LOCHNER TO MRS. DOLAN: THE 20th CENTURY

Abandonment of Property Rights

Although it had produced strong economic growth, Lockean "substantive due process" began to be abandoned in the Theodore Roosevelt administration at the turn of the 19th to the 20th century. Roosevelt and his Progressives wanted to use government to do good and believed that industrial development demanded the establishment of some new rights and some restrictions on individual freedom not contemplated by the Framers or the writers of then-existing law. Principled civil servants would replace politicians in making regulations.

Citizens tend to be aware of the First Amendment's protection of free speech and practice of religion, and of the Second Amendment's right to keep and bear arms. Fewer people are aware of the "takings clause" of the Fifth Amendment to the Constitution, which says, "nor shall private property be taken for public use without just compensation"; yet protection of rights in property is the very reason and justification for the creation of government.

The other rights, freedom of speech, religion and assembly, are mostly to protect us against the government we created to protect property.

The cases arising from the Progressive program began to arrive at the Supreme Court a few years after **Lochner**. The Court's abandonment of the Constitution began with **Village of Euclid v. Ambler Realty Co.** in 1926, the first zoning case — one involving a local ordinance, not a federal law. Richard Epstein, an expert on property law, notes that Ambler Realty owned 68 acres in the 14-square-mile Village, and none of the rest of the area was restricted. A little more than a third of Ambler's property was limited by the ordinance to residential construction, though it could have been developed for valuable commercial use because it was in the path of commercial development. The ordinance reduced its value by 75%, so there was a taking of property which should have been compensated. The trial judge correctly regarded it as a transfer of wealth from one set of landowners to another under the guise of regulation.

The Supreme Court, however, said that exclusion of commercial buildings bore a rational relation to health and safety — such as possible injury to children. It noted that repair of streets might be rendered easier and less expensive by confining the heavy traffic to the business streets. This ignored the fact that the owners had strong incentives to separate the commercial and residential areas to create a community amenity, and that it could design the development so as to route commercial traffic away from residences and to employ more durable materials in building the streets that trucks would use.

The zoning was not necessary for another reason: the

neighbors could have gotten injunctions against development potentially damaging to them. If they were actually damaged, they could sue for damages. It is sometimes objected that individuals cannot afford to sue developers, but it is usually possible for several parties to join in the suit and so spread the cost; or to work with a property-rights legal organization.

No compensation was awarded for the reduction in value of Ambler Realty's property.[ii] (Since then, the Court has allowed takings of up to 95% of a property's value, saying that as long as there is any remaining economic value, there is no taking). The decision was wrong, because under the Fifth Amendment a taking must be for a public purpose, and it must be compensated, because takings without compensation put costs that should be shared by all on a few people selected by the law. An example is when, to protect watersheds, an ordinance "down-zones" from an allowed one house per acre to one per two or more acres. This may reduce the value of the land substantially. A few landowners are made to pay for the protection of the public's water, whereas the cost should be shared by all of them.

Law professor Bernard H. Siegan points out that "Zoning . . . is essentially prior restraint on a use of property that poses no threat of nuisance . . . Thus, zoning authorities are censors, with the power of government to force their ideas on the public."

"Rational Relation" Doctrine

With **Euclid**, the US Supreme Court virtually gave up any effort to monitor legislation in land-use cases. It said that there need only be a "rational relation" to a public purpose, so all such laws cite some public purpose in order to escape scrutiny. This is in contrast to First Amendment cases, in which the Court will strike down a statute unless there is a compelling state interest. In those cases the burden of proof is on the government, where it should be. In Fifth Amendment cases it is on the citizen. A further argument for strict scrutiny of property rights cases is that there can be no freedom of speech where the speaker can be silenced by threats to his property. Developers are often afraid to protest unfair and arbitrary regulation, because they know that they will be treated more harshly by the regulators on future projects.

Nebbia v. New York, in 1934, allowed a state commission to set milk prices. In 1931 and 1932 the prices had gone below the cost of production, and the legislature adopted a statute effectively making the milk business a public utility with a three-member control board to regulate the industry and set retail prices. The board had to figure a "reasonable return" to the farmers and dealers. The primary aim was to improve the economic condition of farmers, and the way they did it was to make it illegal to sell for less than nine cents a quart at retail. Mr. Nebbia sold two bottles of milk and a loaf of bread for eighteen cents and was convicted of a misdemeanor. The Supreme Court upheld the conviction, five to four. It rejected the standard of the previous 150 years and held that due process demands only that the law not be unreasonable or arbitrary and that it have a substantial relation to the objective.

Justice McReynolds wrote for the four-member minority. He wanted to determine whether justification, such as an emergency, existed for depriving Nebbia of his Fourteenth Amendment rights. The minority concluded that shortages are not emergencies justifying intervention by the legislature:

The Legislature cannot lawfully destroy guaranteed rights of one man with the prime purpose of enriching another, even if for the moment this may seem advantageous to the public. . . . The ultimate welfare of the producer, like that of every other class, requires dominance of the Constitution, and zealously to uphold this in all it parts is the highest duty intrusted to the courts. . . . Not only does the statute interfere arbitrarily with the rights of the little grocer to conduct his business according to standards long accepted — complete destruction may follow; but it takes away the liberty of twelve million consumers to buy a necessity of life in an open market. It imposes direct and arbitrary burdens upon those already seriously impoverished with the alleged immediate design of affording special benefits to others. To him with less than nine cents, it says — You cannot procure a quart of milk from the grocer although he is anxious to accept what you can pay and the demands of your household are urgent! A superabundance; but no child can purchase from a willing storekeeper below the figure appointed by three men at headquarters! And this is true although the storekeeper himself may have bought from a willing producer at half that rate and must sell quickly or lose his stock through deteriorations. The fanciful scheme is to protect the farmer against undue exactions by prescribing the price at which milk disposed of by him at will may be resold . . . Grave concern for embarrassed farmers is everywhere; but this should neither obscure the rights of others nor obstruct judicial appraisement of measures proposed for relief.

The majority ignored this argument, saying that under existing circumstances it was not unreasonable for the state to deny Nebbia the liberty to sell milk at his chosen price.

The New York law negated the rights of the people, as Justice McReynolds had pointed out in eloquent language. He showed that economic rights protected them. Law professor Siegan notes that it raises the question of whether Holmes and Brandeis were really the heroes of the Court of the end of the 19th century and the beginning of the 20th. Harlan, McReynolds, Sutherland, Bradley, Pitney and other upholders of Lockean rights may have a better claim to that title. Holmes and Brandeis sometimes seemed to be pushing the Progressive agenda — with no better claim to heroism than some on the next Court who pushed the New Deal agenda, and less than those who had pushed *laissez faire*, which essentially holds to the spirit of the Constitution.

In 1937, by a 5-4 majority, the Court upheld a state statute that established minimum wages for women and minors. It was an infringement on the right of contract and of due process, but in respect to that, Washington State law (in **West Coast Hotel v. Parrish**) determined that the law was a reasonable exercise of legislative discretion, because of the difficult economic conditions and "the unparalleled demand for relief." Justice Sutherland countered that the meaning of the Constitution does not change with the ebb and flow of economic events.

Justice Hughes rejected the belief that the common good is predicated on individual freedom and equated liberty with the application of the police power. Hughes wrote: " . . . the liberty safeguarded is liberty in a social organization which requires the protection of law against the evils which menace the health, safety, morals and welfare of the people. Liberty under the Constitution is thus necessarily subject to the restraints of due process, and regulation which is reasonable in relation to its subject and is adopted in the interests of the community is due process." Due process requires a trial, but not, apparently, in the opinion of Justice Hughes.

He foreshadowed much of modern legal thinking which, unlike Locke and the Constitution, puts community ahead of the rights of the individual, and he added morals and public welfare to the traditional health and safety police-power justifications, thus allowing virtually any regulation to come under it.

Activist judges seized on this and expanded the scope of regulation while weakening individual rights.

In **Olsen v. Nebraska,** in 1941, the Supreme Court unanimously upheld a state statute limiting the fees that private employment agencies could charge. Justice Douglas said that the state did not even have to demonstrate any evils that persisted in the field despite competition. The only suggestions for invalidation of the legislation are "those notions of public policy embedded in earlier decisions of this Court . . ." He meant the "substantive due process" decisions, but while they may have upheld "notions of public policy," they were based on the Constitution. Justice Black wrote that "Under this constitutional doctrine the due process clause is no longer to be so broadly construed that the Congress and state legislatures are put in a strait jacket when they attempt to suppress business and industrial conditions which they regard as offensive to the public welfare."[iii] So there, as in Justice Hughes' **West Coast Hotel** decision, "public welfare" is being used to justify abandoning due process and opening the gates to universal regulation of private property and of the right to contract.

Substantive Due Process Ends

The era of "substantive due process" had come to an end. The Court would no longer overrule legislatures on the basis of natural economic rights, which had been supreme civil rights from the Declaration of Independence onward. Now, instead of putting the burden of proof on government to justify the taking of rights in property, it put the burden on the citizen to show why they should not be taken.

In no other area has the Court extinguished a set of fundamental rights. On the other hand, it has created rights not in the Constitution, such as the right to travel and the right to marital privacy. The latter was constructed by Justice Douglas in **Griswold v. Connecticut** (1965), from "penumbras of specific guarantees of the Bill of Rights formed by emanations from those guarantees that help give them life and substance"[iiii] — in other words, from shadows (penumbras) from the light (emanations) of the Constitution, rather than from its words and the intent of the Framers. This follows the Supreme Court practice through much of the 20th century of making law to achieve desired social ends, when the Congress will not pass the laws. The Court in **Griswold** might have reached the same result by relying on the right of the birth-control clinic in question to contract with its clients, or its property rights in its business — rights actually in the Constitution. But if it had upheld property rights in a social issues case, it would have had to do it in economic cases, which it didn't want to do. It made up law, instead.

Some think that the Constitution should change to accommodate the politics of the times. It must not, for that view has dismantled the rule of law. Some legal commentators believe that the Court cannot go back to the rulings of the Old Court upholding economic rights, because the principle of *stare decisis* ("let the decided matter stand") means that the decisions since

1976 restricting property rights must stand. This is not persuasive, because the Supreme Court has reversed itself many times and can do so in respect to economic rights. It must do so, because its decisions must be based on the words and intent of the Constitution — else why have a written one?

Abandonment and Restoration

Is John Locke's legacy, then, extinguished? To a great extent it is, though the Supreme Court in recent years has edged toward a restoration of property rights. In **First Evangelical Lutheran Church v. Los Angeles** (1987), it said that development moratoria, where government has arbitrarily postponed development, can effect takings, which must be compensated. The **Nollan v. California Coastal Commission** (1987) ruling was that regulations must have a close relationship with the laws in question , and, in **Lucas v. South Carolina Coastal Council** (1992), that regulations that deny the property owner all "economically viable use of his land" require compensation (they can take 95%, but not all).

The Supreme Court signaled its readiness to enforce anew property rights in a 1994 case, **Dolan v. City of Tigard,** in which Mrs. Dolan argued that the City's requirement for a bicycle path on her plumbing and electrical supply store property was not related to the proposed development, and that it was an uncompensated taking of her property. The Court agreed with her. It gave an important reminder of Locke's doctrine when it said: "One of the principal purposes of the Takings Clause is 'to bar Government from forcing some people alone to bear public burdens which, in all fairness and justice, should be borne by the public as a whole'."

The most hopeful statement in the **Dolan** decision was this: "We see no reason why the Takings Clause of the Fifth Amendment, as much a part of the Bill of Rights as the First or Fourth Amendment, should be relegated to the status of a poor relation in these comparable circumstances." The Court was righting the Constitution — perhaps signaling its readiness to reverse **Euclid, Carolene Products,** and the other New Deal decisions. There is to be no more two-tier review system with property rights in second place. They are to be as protected as free speech. Locke's principles are to be respected, because they are in the Bill of Rights.

The Supreme Court followed up on its **Dolan** decision in a 2001 case, **Palazzolo v. Rhode Island,**ᵛᵛ where it reversed lower courts and ruled that they must consider whether there was a partial taking of value of his 18 acres of salt marsh. It could result in requirement of compensation for partial regulatory takings.

In the 1995 **US v. Lopez** decision, a Commerce Clause case, the Supreme Court rejected the argument that Congress needed only a minimum-scrutiny "rational basis" for a federal law against possession of firearms on school properties. The Court said that such possession is not an act in interstate commerce, even though the guns may have moved in such commerce. This reversed the ruling in the above-mentionedcase where a farmer's production of a few acres of wheat for his personal use, which caused him to exceed his quota, was ruled to be a violation of federal law because, while it did not move in interstate commerce, it "affected" it.ᵛᵛ A rational-relation-to-a-public-purpose argument has also been used repeatedly to allow Congress to restrict people's rights in their property, so it seems likely that the Court will reject such arguments in the future.

The Chief Justice noted in **Lopez** that "it is difficult to perceive any limitation on federal power under the government's theory, and Justice Thomas said that the dissenters could not come up with "even one example" of an activity beyond the reach of Congress. The Constitution has been reduced to a single phrase: the General Welfare clause, wrongly interpreted, as Jefferson prophesied.

If the Court continues to reinstate strict scrutiny of economic rights, the cost of living will be lower, the poor wealthier and the economy stronger. Economic over-regulation is a drag on the economy and injures the poor more than others, because it reduces opportunity under the law, which they need more than do others.

A more compelling reason for strict scrutiny of property rights is that John Locke's Natural Law and the Common Law still stand behind the Declaration and the Constitution. The phrases "due process of law," "privileges or immunities of citizens of the United States," "equal protection of the laws" and "nor shall private property be taken for public use without just compensation" are still in our Supreme Law.

Fallacy of the "Living Constitution"

The Constitution is not "a wonderfully flexible document," as has sometimes been claimed. To the contrary, it is wonderfully inflexible, because it is specific in the powers it grants to the federal government. Notes the dean of constitutional scholars, Harvard's Raoul Berger: "The Founders resorted to a written constitution the more clearly to limit delegated power, to establish a 'fixed' constitution alterable only by amendment. A key means for accomplishment of that purpose was their use of common law terms of established and familiar meaning." He notes that Justice Harlan said: "When the Court disregards the express intent and understanding of the Framers, it has invaded the realm of the political process to which the amending power was committed..."[iii]

Some argue that we have a "living" Constitution, which changes with the Common Law. Within a very few years of adoption of the Constitution the argument was being made that the courts can find new meanings and rights in it. James Madison refuted that in a letter to Henry Lee in June, 1824:

> ... I entirely concur in the propriety of resorting to the sense in which the Constitution was accepted and ratified by the nation. In that sense alone it is the legitimate Constitution. ...

To Peter DuPonceau, in August of that year he wrote:

> A characteristic peculiarity of the Govt. of the U. States is, that its powers consist of special grants taken from the general mass of power, whereas other Govts. possess the general mass with special exceptions only ...

He noted that it cannot be supposed that the Convention

> ... which framed it with so much deliberation, and with so manifest a purpose of specifying its objects and defining its boundaries, would, if intending that the Common Law shd. be a part of the national code, have omitted to express or distinctly indicate the intention; when so many far inferior provisions are so carefully inserted ... Nor can the Common Law be let in through the authority of the Courts ... every

plea for an irregular one [channel of interpretation] is taken
away, by the provident article in the constitution
[amendment] for correcting its errors & supplying its
defects. . .

To Thomas Jefferson laws in general, and constitutions in
particular, were shields against tyranny. He said, "To take a single
step beyond the boundaries thus specially drawn around the
powers of Congress is to take possession of a boundless field of
power, no longer susceptible of any definition."[iiii]

The only permissible way to rewrite the Constitution is
through the difficult route of amendment, which requires
concurrence of two-thirds of both houses of Congress and three-
quarters of the state legislatures, or it requires a new
constitutional convention called by two-thirds of the states and
ratified by three-fourths of them. It is not the job of the Supreme
Court to do it, however gradually; but rather to rule on the
validity of laws in light of the words and intent as the Framers
meant them, as Madison explained.

The Butler Case

We lost some of the rights John Locke bequeathed us — guaranteed in the Bill of Rights — through our failure to insist on them and the Supreme Court's failure to protect them. The Court rewrote the Constitution in a series of cases from 1926 through the 1970s, regardless that the Framers' prescribed method for change was amendment.

In the **United States v. Butler** decision in 1936 the Court removed the Article I, Section 8 restrictions on Congress' powers to tax and spend and opened the way to the welfare state, ironically in the process of ruling unconstitutional the New Deal's Agricultural Adjustment Act. James M. Beck, legal scholar and former solicitor general, likened the **Butler** decision to the collision of the ocean liner "Titanic" with an iceberg. "After the collision, which was hardly felt by the steamer at the time, the great liner seemed to be intact and unhurt, and continued to move. But a death wound had been inflicted under the surface of the water, which poured into the hold of the steamer so swiftly that in a few hours the great ship was sunk." While it took years to recognize it fully, the Constitution had been nullified, and the liberties and welfare of the people had been grievously wounded.

"Footnote 4"

The erosion of rights occurred not only in **Butler** but over the course of a number of cases in the Progressive and New Deal eras. A turning point was "footnote 4" of the US Supreme Court's **United States v. Carolene Products** decision in 1938. In it, property rights were suggested to have lower status than other rights, which set a precedent the Court has followed for many years. These two are examples of apparently minor, and at the time almost unnoticed, changes in interpretation which were seized upon by succeeding Courts and politicians to change the nature of government to something quite different from that which John Locke and the Founders had designed. Alexis de Tocqueville, observer of America in the early 19th century, predicted that if we lose our liberty, it will be bit by bit. The great rights and restrictions on government were not lost suddenly; it was a gradual process. The most pronounced changes were in the New Deal, and the changes it made will be described.

Events Leading to the Loss of Rights

Americans should know about the rights we had, those we lost, and how we lost them. To this end it is useful to review some economic and constitutional aspects of United States history beginning with the origins of the 1930s economic depression, because it brought on the New Deal.

Two wrong government policies had played a key part in starting the downturn: currency inflation by the Federal Reserve, and high tariffs imposed by Congress. The attempted remedies for these mistakes were prime examples of how government can create problems and compound them by more intervention, rather than by letting millions of minds work out solutions through private contracts.

Historian Paul Johnson explains that the United States in the 1920s should have followed an internationalist trade policy, but our political leaders did not stand up to protectionist manufacturers and unions. Instead, they sought to keep the world prosperous by deliberate inflation of the money supply. They joined the British financial leaders in what they called "stabilization," the creation of artificial, cheap credit.

Inflation is not caused by a rise in the price of food or of gasoline or of any other commodity or service, because if the money supply is kept constant, when one price goes up others have to fall to compensate. It is caused by government creating more money than there was before to represent the "basket" of goods and services. Only government can cause inflation.

Creation of cheap credit seemed to work for a while in the 1920s. Trade perked up, but it became more and more difficult for the financial managers, led by Governor Benjamin Strong of the New York Federal Reserve Bank, to maintain growth based on inflation. With American productivity growing, prices should have fallen, but they did not because of the inflation. Strong tried a last credit push, which was described by a member of his Board as "the greatest and boldest operation ever undertaken by the Federal Reserve System [and which] resulted in one of the most costly errors committed by it or any other banking system in the last seventy-five years."

The artificial growth effects petered out at the end of 1928 and the economy went into decline six months later, because money did not represent the same real value as before. The market collapsed, and the resulting sharp decrease of the money supply was felt by businesses as a pronounced shrinkage of orders because there were fewer dollars with which to order. The President urged them to retain the workers at their normal pay levels but it was impossible, and they laid off large portions of their work forces.

Harding and the 1920 Recession

A recession was to be expected in the business cycle, though this one was unusually severe because of the degree of government intervention. As Johnson says: It "sorted out the sheep from the goats, liquidated the unhealthy elements in the economy and turned out the parasites . . . business downturns serve essential purposes. They have to be sharp. But they need not be long because they are self-adjusting . . . there was no reason why the 1929 recession should have taken longer than the one in 1920, . . . for the American economy was fundamentally sound." The response by President Harding and Treasury Secretary Mellon to the 1920 recession had been to reduce federal spending by 40% — to get government out of the way — and it was over in a year. Presidents Hoover and Roosevelt extended theirs to twelve years.

In 1929, President Herbert Hoover adopted an interventionist financial policy, deliberately ran a deficit, and combined these measures with bold words and "social engineering": government-directed economic measures.

Our Depression was spread to Europe by the Smoot-Hawley tariff act of 1930, which came on top of the Fordney-MacCumber tariff act of 1922, and imposed such high import duties that our partners could not trade with us. European manufacturers lost business as a result, and with depression overseas America could no longer export. Debt repudiations ensued, foreigners lost confidence in the dollar, and since the US was still on the gold standard they began to pull out their gold. The banking system came to a standstill at the end of Herbert Hoover's presidency.

The Federal Reserve's response should have been to increase the supply of money (as it did successfully and quickly in a similar stock market crash in 1987). The monetary expansion would have been interpreted by business as a renewal of demand for goods and services, which would have created jobs, whose wages would have enabled workers to buy goods and services. It would not have been inflationary, because America's productivity was good — though that was not previously reflected in its money supply. The tariffs should have been repealed immediately by Congress, which would have opened markets for trade and would also have expanded jobs.

FDR Extends the Depression

Hoover's successor, Franklin Roosevelt, abandoned Lockean government. Instead of getting government out of the way, he chose policies in which government would provide jobs and credit. It would abandon the gold standard; it would create programs to "prime the pump" — to put tax money in the hands of individuals who did not earn it. This, it was thought, would revive businesses when they spent it; but it stripped capital from the people who could create jobs. While it created temporary employment, it frustrated long-term employment. It was partly the economic theory of counter-cyclical spending of John Maynard Keynes and partly a speedy way to increase the confidence of the people. It was also a means to build a political coalition through the dispensation of federal funds. Essentially, it was a series of experiments in untested programs that turned out to be ineffective, and often counter-productive, except as confidence-building measures.

Roosevelt did increase confidence, but he did not bring the nation out of the Depression; he extended it ten years (after Hoover's two-year extension), until World War Two, and in the meantime created a recession within a depression. Without Hoover's and Roosevelt's programs, recovery would have been rapid, as it had been in the 1920 recession. There would have been no spending programs to grow gradually out of control and create economic inefficiency and a huge national debt. At least, the programs should have been ended soon, but that seldom happens in government.

Government can make huge mistakes and turn them into prolonged disasters, and the mistaken measures usually involve the abandonment of Lockean property rights that afford the freedom to make intelligent, self-interested change and to correct imbalances reasonably quickly. The people in the market will tend to make the right choices because they will be rewarded, and wrong choices will be punished. Government planners can contribute usefully their ideas for discussion by the market, but they should not be allowed to mandate them.

It was not only legal scholars who held the Lockean view of

property rights before the New Deal. Many, perhaps most, people did; but the mainstream thinking was in process of being changed to support the welfare state. Such beliefs were not to find favor again until another sixty years had passed.

There were many acts of the New Deal that concerned the power to tax and to spend or which bent or abandoned constitutional protections of property rights. President Franklin Roosevelt pushed through ten "relief" laws in the first hundred days of his administration, including the Emergency Banking Act, the Federal Emergency Relief Act, the Agricultural Adjustment Act, the Tennessee Valley Authority Act, and the National Industrial Recovery Act (NIRA).

"Switch in Time Saves Nine"

The NIRA prescribed the drafting and application of "codes" setting prices, minimum wages and maximum hours. Its Title I was declared unconstitutional by the Supreme Court in 1935, because there was no authority for it. Other New Deal laws were struck down, so Roosevelt proposed to "pack" the Supreme Court with additional judges who would do his bidding. The idea was very unpopular and he did not do it, but two justices switched position in the **Jones and Laughlin** case when it was held over for a term — the famous "switch in time that saved nine." It was in this period that **United States v. Carolene Products** came before it. While this case was nominally about milk, it had a long-term effect on rights in property.

Carolene's competitors were having shipment of its "filled milk" (skimmed milk mixed with non-milk fats) outlawed in interstate commerce to rid themselves of its competition. Carolene sued. The Court said that it would not scrutinize the law strictly to see if due process had been followed in depriving Carolene of its rights in its property. Justice Stone's majority opinion said in part: "... regulatory legislation ... is not to be pronounced unconstitutional unless in the light of the facts made known or generally assumed it is of such a character as to preclude the assumption that it rests upon some rational basis within the knowledge and experience of the legislators ..." His now-famous Footnote 4 set up a two-level scrutiny — relegating property rights to the lower level (where a property regulation would be sustained if a "reason" was stated by the legislature) and elevating all others to the higher one where the government had to show a compelling interest to take individual rights. The footnote said:

> There may be narrower scope for operation of the presumption of constitutionality when legislation appears on its face to be within a specific prohibition of the Constitution, such as those of the first ten Amendments ... Nor need we enquire whether similar considerations enter into the review of statutes directed at particular religious ... or racial minorities; whether prejudice against discrete and insular minorities may be a special condition, which tends seriously to curtail the operation of those political processes ordinarily to be relied upon to protect minorities, and which may call for a correspondingly more searching judicial inquiry."

He was suggesting a double standard: a higher scrutiny outside the economic sphere, and a lower one within it. He did acknowledge that subjects falling within the Bill of Rights allowed for "narrower scope for operation of the presumption of constitutionality." Later, the Court would uphold Congress against the Bill of Rights as long as it had a "rational basis."

In contrast, Justice Stewart wrote in **Lynch v. Household Finance** in 1972:

> . . . the dichotomy between personal liberties and property rights is a false one. Property does not have rights. People have rights. The right to enjoy property without unlawful deprivation, no less than the right to speak or the right to travel, is in truth, a 'personal' right, whether the property in question be a welfare check, a home or a savings account. In fact, a fundamental interdependence exists between the personal right to liberty and the personal right to property. Neither could have meaning without the other. That rights in property are basic civil rights has long been recognized. J. Locke, *Of Civil Government*; J. Adams, *A Defence of the Constitutions of the Government of the United States of America*; L. W. Blackstone *Commentaries* . . .

Justice Stone's 1938 footnote in **Carolene Products** eventually became the dictum of the Court, which deferred to Congress rather than to the Constitution. Congress never has difficulty in stating the Court-required "reason" for legislation.

"Tortured" Constitution

President Roosevelt wrote the Ways and Means Committee in 1935 in respect to one of his proposals: "I hope your committee will not permit doubts as to constitutionality, however reasonable, to block the suggested legislation." Rexford Tugwell, a member of his "brain trust" admitted later that: "To the extent that these (New Deal policies) developed, they were tortured interpretations of a document intended to prevent them."

The Ways and Means Committee acquiesced, the Congress did also, and the Court abandoned scrutiny of Fifth Amendment rights and began to uphold laws that did not conform with the Constitution. Americans no longer enjoyed its Locke-inspired liberties. At the same time, First Amendment rights, freedom of speech and religion were given "strict scrutiny," special protection.

15. Locke Makes A Comeback

A Hint of Rights Restoration

We have followed the rights to life, liberty, and the pursuit of happiness from their genesis in Locke's *Second Treatise*, through their institution in our founding documents, through the Federalists' attempts to skirt them right after the Constitution was put in place, and through a century honoring them and drawing strength from them, initiated by Jefferson and his Republicans. We have followed the Progressive intellectuals as they began to abandon the belief in freedom.

The Progressive era gave way to the New Deal, whose "torturing" of property rights and the General Welfare and Commerce clauses was documented earlier. The violations have continued at the hands of Congress, presidents and the Supreme Court. The excuse usually has been that (to paraphrase Elihu Root) the economy and society had changed and that the intervention of government was necessary to produce justice and right conduct, and that new legal rights and obligations were needed that were not contemplated when the Constitution was written. They also thought that disinterested civil servants could carry out the necessary reforms. However, this did not justify abandoning constitutionally-guaranteed rights, and if those were to be altered the proper method was by constitutional amendment. Abandoned they were, with serious consequences to job creation, incomes, and liberty, until the people began to stage a fitful revolution in the voting booths against entrenched special interests near the end of the 20th century.

The renewed interest in John Locke's principles manifested itself approximately on the hundred-year, end-of-century schedule, though it was discernable by 1964 in the campaign of presidential candidate Barry Goldwater. He did not propose to make big-government work better but to reduce its size and influence; but he lost to President Lyndon Johnson.

Spearhead Reformer

When reform came, it was heralded in the late 1970s by a young congressman from New York State, Jack Kemp, who said: "Here in America was the one place on earth where you could climb as far as your abilities could take you. . . . Opportunity, the chance to make it and to improve your life, that's what the American Dream was and is all about. What poisons that dream is when government stands in the way . . . Instead of government serving to create a climate of opportunity, acting as the impartial referee dispensing justice, we now sense that government has become the competition. Our government is the other team — and it's winning!" The reference to government's role as "impartial referee" catches the sense of Locke's philosophy of enforcement of property rights.

Kemp noted that the invention of money gave men the opportunity to continue and enlarge their possessions in different proportions. He advocated economic growth: making the pie larger. Contracts (on which Locke placed such emphasis) are the instruments of economic growth, because in freely made ones both parties gain — or they would not make them.

Kemp had schooled himself in economics. He was the political leader of the "supply-side" economics school, which is the classical economics of Ricardo and Say. As Robert Bartley, editor of *The Wall Street Journal*, paraphrased it: "Supply creates its own demand. That is, manufacturers pay workers to make widgets, and workers use their pay to buy widgets. Savers lend their money to investors who build widget factories, and the factories' profits go to repay principal and interest. A higher price will call forth more widgets, higher wages will call forth more widget-makers, and higher returns will call forth more investment. Unless the government gets in the way, for example by fixing prices, markets will clear and everyone will live happily ever after."

Marginal tax rates, not average rates, mattered, noted Kemp. The marginal rate is the one on the next dollar you make; and if the government will take most of it, you may not be willing to do the work to make it. The effect of graduated tax rates was graphed by economist Arthur Laffer as a curve like that of the Gateway Arch in St. Louis and became known as the "Laffer Curve," which showed that at a zero tax rate and at the 100% rate the government would get no revenue (at the latter rate people would stop working and earning), and at some low rate in between the tax base would be maximized. Congressman Kemp and Senator Bill Roth of Delaware introduced a bill to reduce taxes by 30% over three years. It was defeated in 1978 but became a feature of Ronald Reagan's campaign and was enacted as his 1981 tax cut, which led to one of the longest, strongest economic expansions in modern history; it has continued through the turn of the century, with only, short, shallow recessions the end of the George H. W. Bush and Bill Clinton terms.

Supply-side was derided by President George H. W. Bush as "voodoo economics" and called dangerous and radical by people who, since they called themselves "liberals," should have been for it because of its grounding in economic freedom. It is tested by millennia of experience. Robert Bartley, editor of the *Wall Street Journal*, noted that it was described in the Book of Genesis where seven fat years were followed by seven lean years caused by Joseph's confiscatory tax policy.

An Economist President

Ronald Reagan knew economics; he had majored in it in college. He knew about Ibn Khaldun, a 14th-century Moslem philosopher who wrote: "In the beginning of the dynasty great tax revenues were gained from small assessments. At the end of the dynasty, small revenues were gained from large assessments." And, said Reagan, "We're trying to get down to the small assessments and the great revenues." He pointed out that President Kennedy, and President Coolidge and his treasury secretary Andrew Mellon, had gotten more revenues from lower tax rates. So he knew very well that cuts in tax rates would stimulate the economy and broaden the tax base. He never claimed that they would increase revenue, but they did.

Ronald Reagan had worked in the movie industry and had been president of the Screen Actors Guild, and he said: "At the peak of my career at Warner Bros., I was in the 94% tax bracket. . . . The IRS took such a big chunk of my earnings that after a while I began asking myself whether it was worth it to keep on taking work. . . . If I decided to do one less picture, that meant other people at the studio in lower tax brackets couldn't work as much either; the effect filtered down, and there were fewer jobs available."

Kemp, Roth, and Reagan persuaded Congress to cut marginal tax rates (not tax take) drastically. Federal revenues increased because of the enlarged tax base, and the wealthy paid a higher share of the taxes, because they were willing to expose more of their money to taxation.

Reform's Results

The results were startling. Real growth hit 3.5% in 1983 and 6.8% in 1984. In 1989 the Federal Government was taking in $391 billion more than in 1981, a 65% increase. From 1982 (when the tax policy began to take effect) to 1990, employment was up 2%; approximately twenty million net jobs were created; there were 85% more non-farm proprietors; manufacturing output grew 48%; exports increased 92%; business equipment investment was up 76%; per capita net income was up 19%; and gross national income had increased 32%*. Locke's philosophy was working; even when imperfectly applied.

* "Reagan's Awesome Economic Boom," Alan Reynolds, *The Wall Street Journal*, May 7, 1991.

Detractors of the tax-rate cuts have tried to paint a picture of the rich getting richer and the poor getting poorer, but what they showed mostly was that single-mother households make less money than those which include fathers, and the welfare state had helped to encourage the single-mother kind. Otherwise, all income groups did better, and Blacks and Hispanics bettered their position more than did White non-Hispanics. A study by the politically neutral Urban Institute tracked families from 1977 to 1986 and found that the poorest 20% of families gained 77% in real income, the richest gained 5%, while the middle groups were in between in real gains — and this mixed in two Carter years, so the increase in the Reagan years was probably more dramatic for the poor.

Although Congress promised President Reagan three dollars in spending cuts for each dollar of tax cuts, it did not make them, and he did not insist. Spending increased by $465 billion in 1989 over 1981 (revenues had increased by $391 billion). Even with the defense buildup (which by the Soviets' own admission hastened their collapse), if spending increases had been held by Congress to the rate of inflation, the deficit in 1989 would have been only $23 billion — not $152 billion; and the budget would have been on the path to balance long before the 1997 presidential-congressional budget deal. Some say that the imbalance was the fault of President Reagan's tax cuts. It clearly was not. The fault was on the spending side, for which Congress was largely responsible (though he shares the blame for not fighting harder against it).

The tax system was getting closer to Locke's view: that each person should pay only his share, a flat tax for the protection of government, though Reagan was still a long way from advocating a flat tax. He was arguing over the size of government, more than its role. As he put it, he was dismantling Lyndon Johnson's Great Society, not the New Deal. His campaign promises included doing away with the Department of Education and some other Federal agencies, but he did not fight for the deletions and, besides, abolishing agencies is not as important as abolishing functions. Even worse, he did not fight for holding spending down to the inflation rate (which would have been enough to balance the budget), and the deficits piled up.

George H. W. Bush's Failures and Successes

In electing Reagan's vice president to the presidency in 1988, the electorate thought it was electing Reagan's policies to a third term, but it was not. George H. W. Bush did not share Reagan's economic philosophy, and he reneged on his "no new taxes" promise, which probably more than anything else lost him the 1992 election (along with his large increase in regulation).

Bush's most important step toward reinstating Locke was in his appointment of Federal Circuit Court Judge Clarence Thomas to the Supreme Court. Justice Thomas gave his support to Locke's Natural Law during his confirmation hearings. He has proved to be one of the most consistent upholders of property rights on the Court. He is beginning to influence other justices and to be in the majority. When he is not, he writes powerful, principled dissents. George W. Bush, elected just two terms after his father left office, said during his campaign that he would appoint justices like Thomas who interpret the Constitution strictly. Such appointments afford the best chance of returning to Lockean government.

Clinton, Technocrat

President Bill Clinton moved in the other direction — no follower of John Locke, he. The budget package in 1993 was full of new spending and increases in taxes, and there were proposals for new regulations. The program that frightened the public most was his health care plan, a technocratic construction in which boards of experts would set the terms, conditions and prices of health care delivery. It violated the right of people to make their own contracts and their right to due process of law, and it was far from the purposes for which Congress was permitted to spend money under Article I, Section 8.

By 1997, Clinton was declaring that "the era of big government is over," but he continued to propose new programs and increased spending. He still wanted to "fix" government, and for government to fix social and economic problems — not to be limited to John Locke's, or the Constitution's, principles.

The Contract with America

The Republican congressional candidates in 1994 packaged their ideas in a "Contract with America," which used Lockean themes, ran on them, and won. The Contract ". . . outlined a vision for America's future and the role of government. That vision seeks to renew the American Dream by promoting individual liberty, economic opportunity, and personal responsibility, through limited and effective government, high standards of performance, and an America strong enough to defend all her citizens against violence at home or abroad."

Its supporters carried out their promise to bring to a vote everything in the Contract, and most of it was passed in the 104th Congress.

The five Lockean principles of the Contract were:
- individual liberty
- economic opportunity
- limited government

- personal responsibility
- security at home and abroad.

Congress pledged itself to pass several procedural measures on the first day of the 104th Congress. The first was to: "Require (that) all laws that apply to the rest of the country also apply equally to the Congress." Most people assumed that they did, but for years it had exempted itself from its own laws, such as those on equal employment opportunity and occupational safety. Making legislators subject to the laws they have made is a principle of obvious validity, stated by Locke; but it had been violated by legislators who thought they could arrogate to themselves the privilege of flouting the laws they prescribed for others.

Regulation, the Hidden Tax

While the entire Contract with America was based on Locke's principles, property rights restoration was prominent and was concentrated under the heading: "Roll Back Government Regulations and Create Jobs" — a tax and regulation reduction program. Lowering taxes leaves more money in the hands of those who made it and thereby gives them more choice (freedom of contract) and provides the investment funds to create jobs.

Congress has followed a practice of passing regulatory laws in general language and leaving it to civil servants to specify the actual rules under which individuals will live and work. The result is that the costs often are more than the benefits, and such regulations take rights in property, because they are uncompensated takings. Neither tightly-written regulatory laws nor bureaucratic discretion provides the solution, which lies in limiting government to minimum poli.. power health and safety regulation. The potential gains in jobs, income, and productivity from this would can hardly be imagined, because we have not tried it in a hundred years.

The Contract reckoned that: "The burden of taxes and regulation on investment created an economic 'growth gap' between the historic post-World War II rate of 4% real growth per year to a projection of only 2.5% real growth through the end of this century." They were too pessimistic. The tax cuts and the communications/computer economy hit a high growth rate, partly because the computer industry was so new that there were few regulations to slow it down.

Over-regulation levies a hidden tax. Those who propose regulation (typically on someone else) see benefits for a specific purpose but not the "what is unseen" of 19th century French economist Frederic Bastiat: for example, the unavailability of the money for productive uses. There is often an additional, unplanned ill-effect, such as the increase in fatalities in lighter, less-crash-resistant automobiles designed to meet Congressionally-mandated higher gasoline mileage standards; or gasoline shortages resulting from price controls; or the weakening of families by the welfare system.

Aviation safety is a good example. The public has the impression that government protects it in the air. Actually, probably 90% of safety comes from the facts that pilots like to stay alive (and therefore fly safely and make sure their planes are well-maintained), and that an airline's stock takes a beating in the millions of dollars when one of its planes crashes. (That is a type of "fine" much swifter and stronger than those of government.) The last 10% of protection that comes from government regulation is very costly to the consumer (in all fields, not only aviation).

What It Costs Us

A study exploring regulatory benefits and costs began with a simple measure of the explosion: the length of the annual Federal Register, in which all new regulations must be published, increased from 53,376 pages in Ronald Reagan's last presidential year to 67,716 in 1991. For 1999, under Clinton, the total was 73,879. In Reagan's last year 104,360 Federal employees issued and enforced regulations, while in George H. W. Bush's last year there were 124,994, and the expenditures on regulation under Bush increased 18%, from $9,558 billion to $11,276 billion (measured in 1987 dollars). The cost of administering Federal regulations was nearly $13.6 billion annually.

The study estimated that even after subtracting the benefits of regulation, the net direct costs are $364 billion to $538 billion per year, or between $3,762 and $5,561 per household annually. Other studies suggest that the indirect costs owed to reduced productivity and innovation are greater than the direct costs. Even assuming that the indirect costs amount only to 100% of direct costs, the total cost of regulation, in excess of all benefits, could be $1,656 billion per year, or about $17,000 per household.

Laffer and Bord note several effects of regulation:

(1) It raises prices to consumers and thereby lowers living standards.

(2) It lowers wages and increases unemployment.

(3) It increases uncertainty for business and reduces investment.

(4) It impairs innovation.

(5) It imposes especially heavy burdens on small and medium-sized businesses.

(6) It increases federal and state budget deficits by reducing economic growth and shrinking the tax base.

And it reduces liberty and takes property without compensation. When government acts contrary to Locke's principles, it tends to produce bad results.

A Better Way

Some examples of regulatory issues with the dispositions indicted by Locke and the Constitution:

(1) Issue: A farmer in California was told that he must not cultivate his farm, because it endangered a species of rare rats. The federal government specified penalties for farming, but offered no compensation.

The farmer must be compensated for maintaining a public rat-preserve, per the Fifth Amendment's "just compensation" clause. Otherwise, he loses his farm and his living to benefit the public, which has decided through its representatives that the rats must be saved.

(2) Issue: An employer must by federal law give "family" leave to its employees who have babies (and to other employees under certain circumstances). As a result, a 45-year-old woman in the firm who will have no more babies cannot negotiate hours, pay and benefits to suit her own situation.

The woman and her employer cannot be impaired in employment negotiations by their government; they are guaranteed freedom of contract and choice over terms of employment. If she wants to apply more than her individual power in contract negotiations, she can join a union. Aside from the legal issue, the company, which has to budget replacements for the people on family leave, may no longer have the flexibility to accommodate her needs, so for each woman who can use "family leave," many workers like her are disadvantaged by the law.

(3) Issue: A business is willing to offer a number of summer jobs below the minimum wage — but not at or above it.

The minimum-wage law violates the employer's rights in his business and the employees' rights to bargain for their labor and is an impairment of the right of the parties to contract freely. The practical effect of the minimum wage is that people are not offered jobs and have difficulty climbing the first rungs on the ladder of employment.

(4) Issue: A man wants to broker real estate for a living but cannot, without a license from the state.

Locke said that the fruits of one's labor are his property. The privilege of pursuing a career without government's permission was declared a principal reason for founding the United States of America ("pursuit of happiness" in the Declaration of Independence). A state cannot require licensing in an occupation that does not closely affect health and safety.

(5) Issue: A man whose only capital asset is his automobile is prohibited by his city government from using it as a "jitney," a part-time taxi. The city council permits only franchised taxis, citing public safety. (The real reason his jitney is barred is that the taxi companies don't want lower-priced competition).

The jitney driver cannot be forced out of business. Safety can be protected through mechanical   inspections and driver licensing and bonding, not business licensing.

(6) Issue: A couple wants to build a "granny" cottage on the rear of their lot. The neighbors don't mind, but the zoning does not permit it.

The municipality must allow the granny cottage. Unrestricted use of their property is a basic right, as long as they are not damaging anyone else, which they are not, as attested by the neighbors.

(7) Issue: A city re-zones its reservoir's watershed to permit landowners in it to develop only one house per two acres, instead of the one per acre previously allowed.

The city is taking the property owners' life savings to spare its thousands of taxpayers from paying a little bit each to buy the development rights to protect their drinking water. In this case, if we assume there is a provable market for the previously-permitted higher density, the ordinance will reduce value by $10,000 per acre so for each 100 acres it must pay $1 million, or it must let them develop at one house per acre (or at the market density, according to a 2001 Supreme Court opinion). Otherwise, there is a taking under the Fifth Amendment.

(8) Issue: People downwind of a chemical factory ask for damages for provable liability for respiratory ailments and an injunction against any more discharges into the air.

The polluter must stop fouling the air and compensate those downwind who can prove that their ailments were caused by the factory.

(9) Issue: A man claims he can do "whatever he damn-well pleases" with his land, and it pleases him to have a stinking hog farm with uncontrolled waste runoff near a housing subdivision.

The hog farmer can't do as he pleases when it damages his neighbors. He must clean up the mess, and compensate them.

(10) Issue: A taxpayer wants the Federal government to stop funding agricultural and business subsidies and grants for the arts.

The taxpayer has a valid complaint: agriculture, business, arts, and other programs are not permitted objects of spending by Congress under Article I, Section 8 of the Constitution. (They are not programs for protection of life, liberty and estates.)

A proper regulatory regime would make sure that regulations are imposed only for compelling cases of public health and safety (the justification to regulate under the "police power"), where benefits exceed costs, and compensation is paid where regulations take money and other property.

Government is Poor Help for the Poor

Many assume that government offers the only avenue through which the poor can get financial help, but it is not the only one; and it is the least effective. This chapter and the next describe a Lockean system of private-contract charities to help the poor, combined with increased private sector strength to provide jobs for them. The jobless can get enough private charitable help, provided the potential contributors are lightly taxed.

Lowering taxes and changing from public to private charity would not only increase private contributions but would substitute efficiency for inefficiency in welfare aid. The volunteer sector is a huge factor in helping people who have low incomes, and it could be much larger. All good private agencies have methods to insure the effectiveness of their spending. For example, United Way funding committees make the volunteer relief agencies justify line item budgets. The agencies spend them on the recipients responsibly, efficiently and philanthropically. The money is raised locally, the panels know their communities, and the relief agencies know the poor and how best to help them. It is difficult to fool them. Not all organizations are as reputable as United Way, so it is up to contributors to check out how their money is being used. If it is not being spent well, they can give to another cause or agency — a choice they do not have with their tax dollars.

United Way of America estimates that about 85% of the contributions given to good volunteer agencies actually get to the needy (compared with the Federal Government's probable 45%-or-less efficiency in delivery). According to Independent Sector's "Giving and Volunteering in the United States, 1999, Executive Summary," contributions of donating households averaged $1,075. They gave a total of $135 billion, reported the American Association of Fundraising Council's "Giving USA, 1999." In addition to the contributions of money, 109.4 million people volunteered their services in 1998, which represents 55.5% of the population. Including formal volunteering with agencies and informal activities such as baby-sitting, they put in 19.9 billion hours, worth $226 billion.

The $135 billion in contributions, added to the $226 billion worth of time, is $361 billion from volunteers for the year. The federal budget for 1999 allocated roughly $25 billion to the Department of Health and Human Services (HHS), which handles many of the types of services on which volunteers work. Thus, the volunteer sector's contribution far exceeds it — even though much of people's money goes to taxes and therefore is not available for private charity. If it were, charity should easily be able to replace federal welfare, plus a lot of state welfare spending. In fact, because the efficiency of private charity spending is roughly twice that of the federal government's, it would require only another $12.5 billion or so of private charity to be as effective as HHS's $25 billion budget. The $12.5 billion should not be difficult to raise from people who can choose how to dispose of the money they make. (The numbers will change in future years, but the public/private relationship will generally hold true). The next chapter proposes an excise or flat tax to raise a small, constitutionally-justified budget that would leave about 16% more of households' money in their pockets, roughly $5,000 to $10,000 annually.

Until the early 20th century, charity was a private matter. There were thousands of private agencies designed to meet local needs, supplementing what families and friends did for each other. Charity societies existed in 154 cities, and they had application procedures, they required references, conducted interviews, and kept records to avoid fraud. One of these organizations handled the recovery of Chicago from its disastrous fire in 1871, while the City government's role was primarily to keep order.

Charitable giving does not depend on its tax deductibility. If taxes were reduced, people would contribute more to charity, as they did throughout the Reagan years of lower taxes and regulation. Giving increased dramatically after the Kemp-Roth tax cut in 1981, and by 1990 per capita giving in constant dollars was 50% higher than it had been in 1982. Contributions as a percentage of personal income rebounded during the Reagan years to the levels they held during the Kennedy tax cuts — after having dropped in the intervening years of high taxation.

From Public to Private Charity

Changing from public to private charity will require difficult adjustments. Leadership from the president and governors will be necessary to explain the need to contribute and to point out to the people that the cuts in taxes give them the ability to do so. Existing philanthropic organizations will have to expand, and some new ones will have to be created. There will be "horror stories" (although few resulted from the 1996 "Workfare" program that was replacing welfare). The adjustments will be made and a better welfare system will result. Americans are a compassionate people will respond — especially if taxes are cut and far more money is left in their pockets.

There are congressional proposals to allow tax credits for charity devoted to the poor. This may be a good way to spur donations as long as the present income tax structure is in place, but it is conservative social policy replacing liberal. Under a low, flat tax, tax credits should not be necessary, and people would be completely free to make their own choices. That is what Locke and the Founders had in mind.

Lowering taxes and changing from public to private charity would not only increase private contributions but would substitute efficiency for inefficiency. This is not all that would happen, though. Another effect of the lower taxes would be to improve the ability of private enterprise to create jobs, so that not as much charity would be needed. The states could provide a "safety net," because they don't have the Federal government's prohibitions against funding welfare programs. The combined effects should more than make up for the forgone federal aid.

The order of effectiveness of measures to help the poor is:

(1) allow individuals and private enterprise to retain their money so as to give them more ability to create jobs;

(2) use the volunteer sector;

(3) use local and state government.

Government Trickles Benefits

The program for job creation conforms to Locke and the Constitution: cut spending, reduce marginal tax rates, reduce regulation, limit Congress to its Article I, Section 8 functions. These are moves toward constitutional government.

Let's examine whether they are practical. The lower marginal tax rate system has been called "trickle-down economics," a pejorative term stemming from a misperception that the well-to-do spend most of their money on lavish living and that companies hold back money from their workers, so that there is only a "trickle" left. Therefore, their income above what is considered reasonable by government should be taken and distributed to others — from those who made it to those who did not.

The facts show otherwise: that it is government that trickles wealth down and private enterprise that showers it on the people. It is a matter of relative efficiency in creating jobs and wealth. The US Bureau of Labor Statistics' "Consumer Expenditure Survey,

1995" found that the poorest and second-poorest quintiles spent more than their income. The third 20% spent 90% of their average $26,129 before-tax income; the fourth spent 76% of their $41,845 average; while the highest 20%, with average income of $84,187, spent only 63%. (The dollar figures will increase in the future owing to inflation, but the percentages of income spent in each bracket should remain roughly the same). The rich don't spend it all on lavish living, and the amount not spent on consumer expenditures by the three highest groups was almost $3 trillion: nearly half of the US economy at the time. This enormous sum was available for savings and investment, which creates jobs.

When money is retained in the private sector and invested by the people who earned it, rather than being taxed, approximately 95% is used to create jobs and wealth for others through investment and private spending. The remainder, about 5%, is returned each year to the owners in the form of dividends or interest for the rent of their capital, and the principal amount plus the interest remains to create more jobs and wealth the next year (so it is virtually 100% efficient in job creation). This doesn't suit most politicians, though, because they don't get credit for handing out the money.

Even money not invested but spent on "conspicuous consumption" helps others. It supplies jobs for the people who build the big houses, the automobiles and yachts, for the workers in fancy restaurants, the vacation industry and everything else on which it is spent. Hedonists might be more useful if they invested more, but they still perform an economic function. In a "punish the rich" mood, Congress a few years ago placed high taxes on expensive yachts. It cost many shipyard jobs and almost killed the boatbuilding industry The legislators realized their mistake and re-pealed the law in time to save some of it.

Federal Job Programs

The US Department of Labor is the key agency in government job-creation efforts. It was reported that for the Job Corps, a Labor Department program, cost per trainee is equivalent to that for a Harvard University education. Under one job training contract, all costs were charged to training even though half were for admini-stration and other items (that is only 50% efficiency), and in one case only 30% went to training and most of the rest to the middle-men who brokered the deal. Seventy percent of Job Training and Partnership Act money is supposed to go for training, but the Labor Department Inspector General's Office says, "the real figure is more like 45%."

So, free-market capitalism is 95 to 100% efficient in creating jobs and income, and efficient volunteer agencies score about 85%, while the Federal government's efficiency is likely 45% or less. There is no social or practical justification for taking income in ex-cess of an arbitrary limit and redistributing it, because the benefits pour down on the labor force when those who make the money spend and invest it. It is government that merely "trickles" them down.

The Low Cost of Constitutional Government

Recent Federal budgets have corrected in the direction of John Locke. They don't reach as far as his vision, though, in which everyone pays his share for the protection of property and no more. In our system it would cover general government, defense, and international affairs.

Total budget authority in Fiscal Year 2000 was almost $2 trillion. If spending were restricted to the enumerated items, as Madison and other Framers would have had it, the Federal budget would have allowed only approximately $360 billion for general government (congress, executive, justice, treasury), defense, and international affairs.

The US Fiscal 2000 Budget (in billions of dollars)	
General Government	$41.6
International Affairs	20.6
Defense	293.3
Total *Constitutionally-Authorized* Budget	$355.5
Total *Actual* Fiscal 2000 Budget	$1,800.0
Source: Budget of the United States, Fiscal Year 2001, Table 32-1. (*Note:* Annual interest on the national debt in this budget year was another $359 billion, little, if any, of which would exist with a constitutionally-limited government.	

The $355.5 billion constitutionally-authorized budget is roughly 20% of the total Fiscal 2001 budget that was actually voted; it could have been funded through a tax of about 3.7% on the $9.7 trillion economy. (As late as 1925, the federal government was spending just 4% of the national product). At that rate, people would retain most of the money they now pay in income tax to invest in enterprises, buy homes, give to charity, or whatever they choose; and to pay state and local taxes. The economy would be stimulated, jobs would increase, much less social-welfare spending would be needed and most of it would be administered through private, non-profit community organizations that know the needs of the recipients and the capabilities of the contributors. This does not mean that public welfare would cease, because some of it would be assumed by the states (whose constitutions do not have the same restrictions as the federal), with the result that taxes would be levied where they are spent, accountability would be increased, and administrative costs would be lowered.

Another benefit of the small budget is that it would reform campaign spending for federal office. Controlling $360 billion, mostly for defense, would hardly be worth raising campaign funds, while the ability to hand out almost $2 trillion obviously is.

Taxes are legal for, among other things, post offices and post roads, and defense. President Eisenhower called his super-highway program: "The National System of Interstate and Defense Highways." He cited as its purpose movement of troops and military supplies, to help it pass constitutional as well as political muster — even though the highways perhaps qualified as post roads.

In trying to justify a broader scope for spending, some people make it a big point that federal aid to the arts, for example, is only a fraction of the cost of an aircraft carrier. But defense is the federal government's primary responsibility, while arts and the others are not even among its purposes and permitted powers.

By this point some readers will be thinking: "But, we've been spending on arts, welfare, education, housing, agriculture and many other things for years; hasn't the Supreme Court approved it?" It has. In the 19th century there was a gradual widening of expenditure purposes (national parks and land grants for colleges, for example), which gathered momentum in the Progressive and New Deal eras. As noted, the **Butler** case was a turning point in which the Court, while ruling on the spending authority of Congress under the Agricultural Adjustment Act (AAA), virtually erased the limitations in the General Welfare clause. It said, in that 1936 opinion, that the Constitution does not limit the power of Congress to authorize appropriations of public money for public purposes.

Power to Tax and Spend

The question is whether Congress has the power to tax and spend only for general government and the objects enumerated in Article I, Section 8; or whether it has a General Welfare spending power independent from them. Alexander Hamilton was of the latter view, and the Supreme Court, in **Butler**, sided with him — although his authority is questionable. As noted above, early in the Convention of 1787 he made a five-hour speech in favor of a constitutional monarchy and the elimination of the states; this was not seconded nor debated, and he was only infrequently at the Convention thereafter, so his knowledge of the intent of the other Framers, their compromises, and their decisions was not first hand. Furthermore, he always said he disagreed with the Constitution. And yet the Supreme Court cited him as the authority.

Said the high Court in the 1936 opinion:

> . . . the grant is that public funds may be appropriated 'to provide for the General Welfare of the United States.' . . . Since the foundation of the Nation, sharp differences of opinion have persisted as to the true interpretation of that

phrase. Madison asserted it amounted to no more than a reference to the other powers enumerated in the subsequent clauses of the same section; that, as the United States is a government of limited and enumerated powers, the grant of power to tax and spend for the general national welfare must be confined to the enumerated legislative fields committed to the Congress. . . . Hamilton, on the other hand, maintained the clause confers a power separate and distinct from those later enumerated, is not restricted in meaning by the grant of them, and Congress consequently has a substantive power to tax and to appropriate, limited only by the requirement that it shall be exercised to provide for the General Welfare of the United States. Each contention has had the support of those whose views are entitled to weight . . . Study of all these leads us to conclude that the reading by Mr. Justice Story (the Hamiltonian position) is the correct one . . . It results that the power of Congress to authorize expenditure of public moneys for public purposes is not limited by the direct grants of legislative power found in the Constitution.

There is an argument that Congress is not limited, and there is an argument that it is; but to interpret laws one must find out why they were passed. That is why we have gone back to Locke and his disciples, our Founders. Sometimes it is difficult to discern "original intent," because various members had various intents, and they compromised. There was no evident disagreement among them, however, about the role of government and of rights. The weight of the history on the subject overwhelmingly supports Madison. The Court found weight on the other side, but it was under pressure from the New Deal Administration to rule its programs constitutional. (As noted above, even New Deal leader Rexford Tugwell admitted that most were not.) President Roosevelt had used the unusual pressure of threatening to "pack" the Court with extra justices who would vote with him, and that won him the support of two justices who had been declaring his legislation unconstitutional. Roosevelt then dropped the proposal.

Hamilton Prevails

With the **Butler** ruling, Alexander Hamilton's ideas prevailed a century and a half after Thomas Jefferson defeated them. James Madison was a leader in the Virginia delegation that laid down the principles that were debated and largely adopted in the Convention. He probably authored them. He attended all of the sessions and took the authoritative notes.

The Founders, following the Common Law and Locke, believed that the General Welfare was promoted by the protection of rights in property. They set up a government limited to the functions necessary to accomplish that purpose — the ones in the limited budget above.

This "strict construction" argument concerning taxes and spending is classic liberalism but is rejected by modern "liberals" (more correctly, statists, or democratic socialists), who say that the nation is different now and needs new laws — even new rights and principles of government. Their view is that the Constitution is a "living" document which must reflect current thinking.

It is not. It was designed to be inflexible concerning rights and principles. As was noted earlier, it is why we have a written one. In spite of this, Supreme Court interpretations of the Welfare and Commerce clauses have given Congress virtually unlimited powers of taxation and expenditure. The Court (in many cases only five justices) has changed the Constitution, notwithstanding its duty to apply the fundamental law's words and intent to legislation. It has unmoored from the Constitution and followed modern political currents.

Constitutional Authority for Bills

Constitutionality would be aided by passing a law requiring that the constitutional authority for every act be cited. Thomas Jefferson thought that Congress should have responsibility for the constitutionality of its acts. Chief Justice John Marshall established his Court's authority as the interpreter.

Citizens might prefer a low excise or flat tax and limited spending. On the other hand, they may no longer be willing to go that far in limiting the Federal government. If not, as noted earlier, taxing and spending powers should be extended by amendment, as provided in the Constitution. That requires a two-thirds vote of both houses of Congress and approval by three-quarters of the state legislatures, not by a handful of justices. The debates on the amendments would be enlightening.

Property Rights Given New Life

Turning from the powers of Congress to property rights, the other principal area of modern Supreme Court misinterpretation, **Dolan v. City of Tigard** in 1994 reinvigorated the Fifth Amendment, the key one in property rights, saying that it is equal to the First and Fourth. This opening can be secured by a president who will appoint "strict construction" justices, and a chief executive of that turn of mind could also veto unconstitutional bills as Pierce, Cleveland and others did. Congress would then have to debate constitutionality in deciding whether to override, and each debate would be an education for legislators and the public and would promote adherence to the Constitution.

Attempted Injunction

One might reason that a citizen would be able to bring suit to stop unconstitutional expenditures by government, and there is a case on this subject, **Frothingham v. Mellon**, which arose in 1923. Mrs. Frothingham sued as a federal taxpayer to enjoin the Secretary of the Treasury from making expenditures under the Maternity Act of 1921, which provided for conditional grants to state programs "to reduce maternal and infant mortality." She argued that the Act was "a usurpation of power not granted to [Congress] — an attempted exercise of the power of local self-government reserved to the States by the Tenth Amendment." She alleged that spending under the Act would increase her tax liability and that she would thereby be deprived of property without due process of law. A unanimous Court held that the suit "must be disposed of for want of jurisdiction," because she "had no such interest in the subject-matter, nor is any such injury inflicted or threatened, as will enable her to sue."

The Court's reasoning was that her

> . . . interest in the moneys of the Treasury (is) shared with millions of others; is comparatively minute and indeterminable; and the effect upon future taxation, of any payment out of the funds, is so remote, fluctuating and uncertain, that no basis is afforded for an appeal to the

preventive powers of a court of equity . . . if one taxpayer may champion and litigate such a cause, then every other taxpayer may do the same . . . in respect of every other appropriation act. . . . The bare suggestion of such a result, with its attendant inconveniences, goes far to sustain the conclusion which we have reached, that a suit of this character cannot be (maintained). The functions of government under our system are apportioned. (We) have no power *per se* to review and annul acts of Congress on the ground that they are unconstitutional. That question may be considered only when the justification for some direct injury suffered or threatened, presenting a justiciable issue, is made to rest upon such an act. . . . The party . . . must be able to show not only that the statute is invalid but that he has sustained or is immediately in danger of sustaining some direct injury as the result of its enforcement, and not merely that he suffers in some indefinite way in common with people generally. . . . Looking through forms of words to the substance of [the] complaint, it is merely that officials of the executive department of the government are executing and will execute an act of Congress asserted to be unconstitutional; and this we are asked to prevent. To do so would be not to decide a judicial controversy, but to assume a position of authority over the governmental acts of another and co-equal department, an authority which plainly we do not possess.

Raoul Berger, distinguished constitutional scholar, did extensive research on the issue of a citizen's standing to sue. He said that,

Not a little of the confusion originated in **Frothingham v. Mellon**, which left uncertain whether "standing" was a constitutional requirement or simply a "rule of self-restraint" . . . "Standing" is not mentioned in the Constitution or the records of the several conventions . . . in the North Carolina convention it was said that "if Congress should make a law beyond the powers and spirit of the Constitution, should we not say to Congress, 'You have no authority to make this law. There are limits beyond which you cannot go. You cannot exceed the power prescribed by the Constitution.'" "Standing to sue" is a judicial construct pure and simple . . . it apparently entered our law via **Frothingham** in 1923.

He traced the issue far back into English law and found that: "Public suits instituted by strangers to curb action in excess of jurisdiction were well established in English law at the time Article III (of the Constitution) was drafted. . . . There may well be policy arguments in favor of a 'personal interest' limitation on standing, but they cannot rest on historically-derived constitutional compulsions."

19. LOCKE'S IDEAS STILL WORK

At the turn of the 20th to the 21st century, there is discussion about the proper *role* of government, not simply about how much to spend on various welfare state programs. Many citizens believe that the federal government is more involved in their lives than it is supposed to be, and previous chapters have demonstrated that this is so, according to constitutional standards.

In the last couple of decades there has been a gradual, uneven movement toward limited government. Whether the people want to return to Locke's model of government as primarily the protector of property, it is too early to say, though sometimes they seem frustrated that sixty years of welfare state rule has not produced good results and has not been overturned more quickly. One of their biggest frustrations is over campaign spending, though it will not be reformed while federal politicians can keep control of $2 trillion of their money; thus the true campaign reform is to limit government to its Lockean role.

US citizens will probably like it more and more as the role of government is limited and they learn how to operate in the new environment. If they don't like it and want to stop short of the original limitations, they can do so by amending the Constitution, but the role may still be smaller than now.

Some will fear the changes. They think the poor will be abandoned; that the nation would be giving up its commitment to education, to the environment; that the arts will wither. On the contrary, all of those will get more effective attention from people who really care because they are improving their property and their lives; because they will be supported by a better economy producing more jobs. Wealthy nations have lower birth rates, so population pressures will be reduced. Private owners are better stewards of resources than governments, because their future and their children's future depends on it. Philanthropy will benefit from the dollars that formerly went to federal taxes, and the states, which do not have the restrictions on their functions that the federal government does, can handle the rest quite well. Their various methods will provide models of the good and the not-so-good and will provide "safety valves" for contentious issues, because there are likely to be states to which people can go that follow practices they prefer.

Following the limited-government model of the Constitution does not imply that the president cannot use the publicity apparatus of his office to make proposals about society and business. This is a legitimate leadership role, even where government may not legislate.

Restoring the Constitution's Primacy

The people can have the liberty won in the American Revolution, if they demand it from their representatives. Or, the Supreme Court can restore it. It's that simple — and that difficult.

Liberal, limited government can only be restored by eliminating the programs and regulations not authorized by the original Constitution or by amendment. The discussion could end here, but it seems useful to be more specific about which programs and agencies are not authorized and to spell out some possible steps toward their elimination.

The proposals are not new, but they shock those who assume that we cannot do without the programs we are used to; there is no one alive who has experienced the original system. The limited system would work better. While it is difficult to prove that it would do so again, it did work for 150 years. It would have prevented the Great Depression by applying Locke's property protections, which tend to promote productive economic results.

There are only two ways to change the present misconstruction: one is by constitutional amendment; the other is through the United States Supreme Court's use of the original intent concerning rights in the Constitution as the basis for its opinions.   T h e objective should be to work toward a federal government, whose taxing and spending functions are enumerated in the Constitution, i.e., the $360 billion budget above for general government, defense, and international affairs, in which taxes and expenditures are strictly for the protection of life, liberty and estates. Individuals, philanthropies and the states should do the rest, and the case is that the people will be far better off with equality of opportunity before the law than with attempted equality of results. The poor, especially, will benefit, because they, more than any, need equal opportunity in order to be able to work their way out of poverty.

Some significant beginnings have been made. There are fewer "entitlements": open-ended commitments to spend. Programs are to be reviewed and re-authorized periodically. The budget is balanced. The debt will not take up increasing amounts of savings and may be retired, so savings can go to job creation. The greatest benefit will come from the reduction in spending, because government spending is inefficient. Even when the budget is in balance, spending will have to be markedly curtailed in order to be constitutional.

Cleaning Up Government Spending

The budget reductions, if any, have been modest. The rate of growth of Medicare is being reduced, but it will still grow. The National Endowments for the Arts and for the Humanities and the Corporation for Public Broadcasting budgets were cut slightly and are increasing again, and that is typical of what will happen to most programs — even after tough talk.

Other functions and agencies should be eliminated because they are extra-constitutional, and it is the functions, more than the agencies, which must be eliminated. This should begin with the Commerce Department — starting with a business agency should make killing others more palatable. Others include: the programs of the Department of Labor; the Education Department (which will save about $55 billion per year and improve education); Veterans' Affairs (unless it is viewed as the continuing obligation to those who served in defense of liberty — if so, convert its benefits to a voucher system); Energy; Agriculture; Housing and Urban Development; most of the Transportation Department (Congress is authorized to spend on post roads, so its Bureau of Public Roads could co-fund a national network with the states and help them in their planning; Health and Human Services; the Environmental Protection Agency (which is overrated as a protector and too often takes property without due process and imposes regulations that cost more than they benefit). There are independent agencies that should be terminated for the same reasons.

Boards and commissions that don't have public health and safety functions should be abolished. The ones that do should be reviewed to see whether they are justified.

Unauthorized Federal taxing and spending functions now in place which are to be continued should be authorized by constitutional amendment. Authorization for national parks would be a relatively non-controversial amendment to be offered for ratification by the states.

Cleaning up the Tax Structure

John Locke said that " . . . it is fit everyone who enjoys his share of the protection (of property) should pay out of his estate his proportion for the maintenance of it." While he did not design a tax system, it is evident that it would be in the nature of a fee for government's protection of life, liberty and estates — the same proportion of each person's wealth: a flat tax. It is also evident that taxes were not to fund anything else, such as the departments, agencies and programs cited for elimination.

The $360 billion budget can probably be financed through excise taxes. If there is to be an income tax, it should be at a flat rate. The flat tax is fair and leaves little opportunity for manipulation by the politically influential. It would have a "family allowance," below which income would not be taxed, and there would be a single tax rate on the rest of income. Business expenses would be deductible. Inventory would be capitalized at the time of purchase. Cost of capital would be an expense. There would not be double taxation, as there is now, with taxes on business and then taxes on the same income in the hands of individuals. Death taxes would be eliminated (no taxation without respiration!). The form to calculate taxes would be very short, and the taxpayer would write a check, so that he or she would be as aware of what was being paid for government as for groceries; there would be no more tax withholding by employers. The tax rate would be low after elimination of the unconstitutional programs. Campaign finance abuses will virtually cease when the budget is not handing out special privileges and subsidies through politicians.

For any other governmental functions, the states should do the taxing. They can pick up any or all of the functions eliminated from the federal government, though philanthropies would undertake many of them. State taxes would have to be increased to pick up the remainder of the programs, but states would be so much more selective and efficient than the federal government that they would not increase them by as much as the federal government cut them. There would be a considerable net gain to the economy. Some think that the states will not do a good job (and some of them will not, at first), but they have an incentive to improve because they compete with each other to attract employers and useful citizens. Providing economic and social alternatives is one of the functions of the federal system performed by the states. They seem likely to do as well as or better than the federal government on the tasks they assume from it.

Reducing Regulation

The cost of over-regulation, it was explained above, is approximately $1 trillion a year; $10,000 or more per family. If the Supreme Court had given strict scrutiny to economic laws for the past sixty years and had required that due process be followed and compensation be paid for takings of property, over-regulation could not have taken place. Congress and government agencies would quickly realize that only the most necessary regulations were worth paying compensation. This conforms with Locke's philosophy that every person must be left "whole" in dealings with government (and whole means *whole*; the Framers were following Locke, and partial takings were intended to be compensated). He said that government cannot take the least part of one's property without one's consent, so the Framers provided that just compensation be paid even when the state could show a compelling need for it.

Regulations should be reviewed regularly to determine whether they are working well in their present forms — or are needed at all. If not, they should "face the sunset."

Adopt benefit-cost provisions. A regulation whose cost to society is greater than its benefits is not justified.

This legislation for balancing the "regulatory budget" would put the government on track toward the goal of minimum health and safety regulation and require annual assessments of the program of regulation. Like tax reduction, it would stimulate the economy. All of the measures on regulation reduction and review will increase and protect individual liberty, the cornerstone of Lockean government and of the Bill of Rights.

Adopt risk-assessment legislation. Regulations should be based on good science and not on emotion and vague possibilities of threats to health and life.

States and local governments should adopt similar provisions. People encounter their regulations more frequently than those of the federal government.

Constitutionality Review

Pass a law requiring that the constitutional authority for each bill be stated, because it would stimulate debate and tend to encourage bills that are constitutional. Review should insure that in committee there is a thorough airing of opinion (especially by constitutional scholars) on the annual tax and appropriations bills, as to whether Congress has authority to levy the taxes and spend the money; and the views should be transmitted to the full House and Senate. Other bills should be subject to review also. Where it is believed that there is no authority for proposed laws, amendments to the Constitution can be offered. That would insure a national debate in which the states will be a part. It will be startling to many that the constitutionality of federal welfare spending, for example, is raised in an appropriations bill, because they have assumed that it is lawful. The debate in Congress and in public forums, the Internet, newspapers, radio and television would be enlightening.

Even with constitutional review, the danger is that those who want to depart from strict construction will, if they are in the majority, simply assert constitutionality. Opposing views must be heard and published.

Presidents should state the constitutional authority for laws in their signing and veto messages.

Conducting these reviews will not diminish the function of the Supreme Court; the Court will have the last word, but the legislative history on the subject will provide guidance to the justices concerning congressional intent. They are less likely to overturn laws where this has been carefully considered. The debates on constitutionality should be given the widest possible dissemination to the public. People need to understand that there are serious constitutional questions, and that Congress cannot simply pass anything it wants — that there are limits on its power for their protection.

The Supreme Court

The political changes outlined above to reestablish Lockean, constitutional government will probably not be made, because of the tenacity with which special interests will fight against them. However, at the Supreme Court the return to first principles is already underway. This is the avenue of reform.

The Supreme Court in **United States v. Lopez** in 1995 gave notice that it planned to restore the Constitution. Said the Court:

> We start with first principles. The Constitution creates a Federal Government of enumerated powers. See Article I, Section 8. As James Madison wrote: 'The powers delegated by the proposed Constitution are few and defined. Those which are to remain in the State governments are numerous and indefinite.' ... This constitutionally mandated division of authority 'was adopted by the Framers to ensure protection

of our fundamental liberties. . . . Just as the separation and independence of the coordinate branches of the Federal Government serve to prevent the accumulation of excessive power in any one branch, a healthy balance of power between the States and the Federal Government will reduce the risk of tyranny and abuse from either front.'

This statement re-establishes Madison's view, repudiates Hamilton's, and signals an intent to restore the constitutional limitations on our Federal Government. While this was a Commerce Clause case, in which the Court limited Congress' powers a bit, the "first principles" statement looms as very important, and the Court has followed up in subsequent decisions.

Congress, as stated earlier, has power to legislate only for the purposes enumerated in Article I, Section 8: to lay and collect taxes, defense, borrow money, coin money, regulate commerce, establish post offices and post roads, rule the District of Columbia, and a few others. The Court's restatement of this presumably means that it intends to strike down taxation and spending which does not conform. This would include laws for agricultural and business subsidies, government-financed medicine, and Federal aid to education, among others. Through cases brought to it over the years to come, the Supreme Court will overturn the welfare clause interpretation in **US v. Butler** (1936) (which, as noted, launched the welfare state), in which the justices had ruled that Congress was not limited by the enumerated powers but had a power separate and distinct under the General Welfare clause. They quoted Alexander Hamilton, who disagreed with the other Framers on this, as on many political issues.

James Madison, "Father of the Constitution," asserted that the

General Welfare clause amounted to no more than a reference to the other powers enumerated in the subsequent clauses of the same section; that, as the United States is a government of limited and enumerated powers, the grant of power to tax and spend for the general national welfare must be confined to the enumerated legislative fields committed to the Congress. The Court in **Lopez** agreed with him and quoted him; thus he was vindicated 60 years after **Butler.**

In the **US v. Morrison** decision in 2000 (on a federal law which intruded on states' legislative powers), the Court built on **Lopez** when it again recognized that the Federal Government is restricted from legislating in areas the Constitution left to the states or the people.

The US Supreme Court will not use **Lopez** to sweep away federal programs. It will rule case by case (**Morrison** being the first), keeping the issues narrow (which, as explained, accounts for the slow cycle of change), perhaps ruling unconstitutional an agricultural subsidy or marketing rule here, a family leave act or minimum wage there, or an export guarantee, or Federal funding for education; and it will limit taxation. The curbs will be gradual enough that there will probably not be great protest at the loss from time to time of a government program or two. There will be time to accept each stage of withdrawal as normal, just as we now think the welfare state is normal after growing it gradually since the **Butler** case in 1936.

The back door route to the welfare state has been regulation, which instead of directly redistributing income transfers valuable rights in property. Through regulation, the property rights of some have been transferred to others without compensation in the value of about a trillion dollars per year, but in 1994 the Court in **Dolan v. City of Tigard,** as has been explained, proclaimed the Takings Clause of the Fifth Amendment as much a part of the Bill of Rights as the First or Fourth Amendments. "One of the principal purposes of the Takings Clause is 'to bar Government from forcing some people alone to bear public burdens which, in all fairness and justice, should be borne by the public as a whole'," *i.e.,* government may not confiscate one person's property and give it to others. The Court seemed to be signaling its readiness to reverse **Euclid** and the New Deal decisions and inviting takings cases through which it can restore strict scrutiny of peoples' rights in their properties (life, liberty, stocks, bank accounts, mortgages, real estate, careers). There is to be no more two-tier review system with economic rights in second place. They are to be as soundly protected as free speech. If good cases are brought, like **Palazollo** in 2001 (a move toward compensation for partial taking), the Court will right the Constitution.

Many people believe sincerely that the welfare state is a better system than that of the Framers, that Article I, Section 8 should not be enforced; but they should not then advocate a "flexible Constitution," or demand appointment of judges who will write the common law into the supreme law. They must follow the amending procedure installed in the Constitution to accommodate changes. We have a political system designed to secure liberty. Certain limited responsibilities are assigned to the federal government and all others are retained by the states or the people. Justices who affirm this and interpret laws accordingly are following the constitutional mandate; those who do not are not, and the future depends on which kind of justices will be appointed.

This book has traced the history of Lockean rights from their installation in our founding documents through US Supreme Court cases for two and a quarter centuries — during which they were first upheld, and then undermined. The outlook in the next century is a hopeful one. The Court has promised to hold to the principles of the Constitution. John Locke, the Declaration of Independence, the Constitution and its Bill of rights may yet prevail. Just as we can hardly remember what government was like in 1900, people in 2100 may scarcely remember the type we have now.

The enterprise which is the United States of America is infused with the spirit of John Locke, philosopher of government. It adopted his concept of a contract to protect citizens' lives, liberties and pursuit of happiness — their "property." A greater idea has not been put forward, nor a better system of government devised.

ENDNOTES

1. Catherine Drinker Bowen. *Miracle at Philadelphia.* (Boston, Toronto: Little, Brown and Company). 1966. pp. 1-292.

2. Claude G. Bowers. *Jefferson and Hamilton.* (Boston and New York: Houghton Mifflin Company. 1925. P. 29.

3. Dumas Malone. *Jefferson the President: First Term, 1801-1805.* (Boston: Little, Brown and Company. 1970. P. 318.

4. Stephen Moore, "The Unconstitutional Congress," *Policy Review* Number 72 (Spring 1995): pp. 22-27.

5. Samuel Eliot Morison. *The Oxford History of the American People.* (New York: Oxford University Press. 1965. P. 401.

6. Stephen Moore. "The Unconstitutional Congress," *Policy Review* Number 72 (Spring 1995): pp. 22-27.

7. Bernard H. Siegan, *Economic Liberties and the Constitution.* (Chicago & London, University of Chicago Press), pp. 112-121.

8. *Ibid.,* p. 111.

9. Samuel Eliot Morison. *The Oxford History of the American People.* (New York: Oxford University Press. 1965. pp. 811-812.

10. F. A. Hayek, *The Constitution as Liberty,* (Chicago and London: University of Chicago Press). 1960. p. 2.

11. Richard A. Epstein. *Takings: Private Property and the Power of Eminent Domain* (Harvard University Press, Cambridge, Massachusetts and London, England. 1985). pp. 131-133.

12. Bernard H. Siegan. *Economic Liberties and the Constitution.* (Chicago and London: University of Chicago Press, 1980). pp. 145-146, 186-187.

13. *Ibid.,* p. 17.

14. *"Supreme Court Strikes a Blow for Property Rights," Wall Street Journal,* July 3, 2001 and "The Earth Rebalanced," *Wall Street Journal,* July 10, 2001.

15. Wickard v. Filburn, 317 US 111, 63 S.Ct. 82, 87 L.Ed. 122 (1942).

16. Raoul Berger, *Selected Writings on the Constitution.* (Cumberland, Virginia: James River Press. 1987. P. 274.

17. Dumas Malone. *Jefferson and the Rights of Man,* Volume Two of *Jefferson and His Time.* (Boston: Little, Brown and Company. 1951). pp. 342-343.

18. Stephen Moore, "The Unconstitutional Congress," *Policy Review* Number 72 (Spring 1995): pp. 22-27.

19. Paul Johnson, *Modern Times, the World from the Twenties to the Nineties,* (New York: HarperPerennial 1992). pp. 236, 246.

20. Bernard H. Siegan, *Economic Liberties and the Constitution,* (Chicago and London, University of Chicago Press. 1980). p. 186.

21. Lynch v. Household Finance Corp., 405 US 538 (1972).

22. Stephen Moore. "The Unconstitutional Congress," *Policy Review* Number 72 (Spring 1995): pp. 22-27.

23. Jack Kemp. *An American Renaissance.* (New York: Berkeley Books. 1981). pp. 1-2.

24. Robert L. Bartley. *The Seven Fat Years.* (New York: The Free Press. 1992). p.49.

25. *ibid.,* pp. 89-90.

26. William G. Laffer III and Nancy A. Bord. "George Bush's Hidden Tax: The Explosion in Regulation." The Heritage Foundation. 1993.

27. "Lessons from the Chicago Fire" by Daniel T. Oliver. *Ideas on Liberty,* February, 2000.

28. Martin L. Gross. *The Government Racket; Washington Waste from A to Z.* (New York: Bantam Books. 1992.) pp. 111-117.

29. United States v. Butler, 297 US 1. (1936).

30. United States v. Lopez, 515 US 55 (1995).

31. United State v. Morrison, Vol. 120, *Supreme Court Reporter,* p. 1740. (2000).

BIBLIOGRAPHY

Books

Robert L. Bartley. *The Seven Fat Years*. (New York: The Free Press, 1992).

Raoul Berger. *Selected Writings on the Constitution*. (Cumberland, Virginia: James River Press, 1987).

Catherine Drinker Bowen, *Miracle at Philadelphia*, (Boston, Toronto: Little, Brown and Company, 1960).

Claude G. Bowers. *Jefferson and Hamilton*. (Boston and New York: Houghton Mifflin Company, 1925).

Warren E. Burger. *It is So Ordered*. (William Morrow and Company, 1995).

George Ticknor Curtis. *History of the Origin, Formation, and Adoption of the Constitution of the United States, Vol. II*, (Harper and Brothers, 1863).

Joseph J. Ellis. *American Sphinx: the Character of Thomas Jefferson*. (Borzoi Book: Alfred A. Knopf, Inc, 1997).

Joseph J. Ellis. *Founding Brothers: The Revolutionary Generat ion*. (Borzoi Book: Alfred A. Knopf, Inc. 2000).

Richard A. Epstein. *Takings: Private Property and the Power of Eminent Domain*, (Harvard University Press, 1985).

Philip S. Foner, Ed. *Basic Writings of Thomas Jefferson*. (Halcyon House, 1944).

Thomas Fowler. *John Locke*, (New York: Harper & Brothers, Publishers, 1880).

David Frum. *Dead Right*. (A New Republic Book, 1994).

Ed Gillespie and Bob Schellhas, eds., *Contract with America* (Times

Books, 1994).

Newt Gingrich. *To Renew America*, (HarperCollinsPublishers, 1995).

Martin L. Gross. *The Government Racket. Washington Waste from A to Z.* (New York: Bantam Books, 1992).

Barry Goldwater. *Conscience of a Conservative*. (Regnery Gateway, 1990).

Gerald Gunther. *Constitutional Law, Eleventh Edition*. (The Foundation Press, Inc. , 1985).

Gerald Gunther. *Learned Hand*. (Pantheon Books), 1993.

F. A. Hayek. *The Constitution as Liberty*, (Chicago and London: University of Chicago Press, 1960).

Burton J. Hendrick. *Bulwark of the Republic: A Biography of the Constitution*, (Little, Brown and Company, 1937).

Philip K. Howard. *The Death of Common Sense*, (Random House, Inc, 1994).

Paul Johnson. *Modern Times, the World from the Twenties to the Nineties*, (New York: HarperPerennial, 1992).

Maldwyn A. Jones. *The Limits of Liberty: American History, 1607-1980*, (Oxford University Press, 1983).

Jack Kemp. *An American Renaissance*. (New York: Berkeley Books, 1981).

William G. Laffer III and Nancy A. Bord. "George Bush's Hidden Tax: The Explosion in Regulation." The Heritage Foundation, 1993.

John Locke. *Of Civil Government*, Second Essay (Chicago, Illinois: published by the Henry Regnery Company for the Great Books Foundation, 1948).

John Locke. "The Second Treatise on Civil Government," *John Locke on Politics and Education*. (Walter J. Black, Inc., 1947).

John Locke. "Some Thoughts Concerning Education," in *John Locke on Politics and Education*. (Walter J. Black, Inc., 1947).

John Locke. "A Letter Concerning Toleration" in *John Locke on Politics and Education*. (Walter J. Black, Inc., 1947).

Pauline Maier. *American Scripture, Making the Declaration of Independence*. (New York: Alfred A. Knopf, Inc., 1997).

Dumas Malone. *Jefferson and His Time*, Volume 1, *Jefferson the Virgin-*

ian, (Boston: Little, Brown and Company, 1948).

Dumas Malone. *Jefferson and His Time,* Volume 2, *Jefferson and the Rights of Man.* (Boston: Little, Brown and Company, 1951).

Dumas Malone. *Jefferson and His Time,* Volume 3, *Jefferson and the Ordeal of Liberty.* (Boston: Little, Brown and Company, 1962).

Dumas Malone. *Jefferson and His Time,* Volume 4, *Jefferson the President: First Term, 1801-1805.* (Boston: Little, Brown and Company, 1970).

Dumas Malone. *Jefferson and His Time,* Volume 5, *Jefferson the President: Second Term, 1801-1805.* (Boston: Little, Brown and Company, 1974).

Dumas Malone. *Jefferson and His Time,* Volume 6, *Jefferson the President: Second Term, 1801-1805.* (Boston: Little, Brown and Company, 1981).

Samuel Eliot Morison. *The Oxford History of the American People.* (Oxford University Press, 1965).

Charles Murray, *What It Means to Be a Libertarian.* (New York: Broadway Books, 1997).

"Lessons from the Chicago Fire" by Daniel T. Oliver. *Ideas on Liberty,* February, 2000.

Howard R. Penniman, *John Locke on Politics and Education.* (Roslyn, NY, Walter J. Black, Inc., Published for the Classics Club, 1947).

Bernard H. Siegan. *Economic Liberties and the Constitution,* (Chicago & London, University of Chicago Press, 1980).

David Wootton. *Political Writings of John Locke.* (London: Mentor, published by the Penguin Group, 1993).

The Book of Common Prayer, "A General Confession" (Oxford University Press, 1928).

Articles

"The Long Road to Tax Reform," by David Brinkley, *The Wall Street Journal,* September 18, 1995.

"Locke and Liberty," by Maurice Cranston, *The Wilson Quarterly,* Winter, 1986.

"Sign Here to Complete the Reagan Agenda," by John R. Kasich, *The Wall Street Journal*, October 18, 1994.

"Splitting with Lopez", by James J. Kilpatrick, *The News and Observer*, Raleigh, NC, Sept. 20, 1995.

Stephen Moore, "The Unconstitutional Congress," *Policy Review* Number 72 (Spring 1995): pp. 22-27.

"Freedom, Responsibility, and the Constitution: On Recovering Our Founding Principles," by Roger Pilon, *Notre Dame Law Review*, Volume 68, Issue 3, 1993.

"Reagan's Awesome Economic Boom," by Alan Reynolds, *The Wall Street Journal*, May 7, 1991.

"The Middle Class Boom of the 1980's," by Alan Reynolds, *The Wall Street Journal*, March 12, 1992.

""Ten Years of Kemp-Roth," by Paul Craig Roberts, *The Wall Street Journal*, August 13, 1991.

Getting Richer (At Different Rates)", by John C. Weicher, *The Wall Street Journal*, June 14, 1995.

"Trashing America's Economy," by Michael Walden, *Carolina Journal*, October-November, 1992.

"Growth's Handmaiden" editorial, *The Wall Street Journal*, September 18, 1995.

"Returning to the Founders' Intent," *The Arizona Republic*, July 15, 1995.

Other Sources

"The Declaration of Independence," reprinted for the Great Books Foundation, Henry Regnery Company, 1948.

The U. S. Bureau of Labor Statistics, "Consumer Expenditure Survey."

The Budget for Fiscal Year 2000, U.S. Government Printing Office.

H.R. 9, 104th Congress, First Session.

Regulatory Transition Act of 1995, H.R. 450, with testimony to the Subcommittee on National Economic Growth, Natural Resources and Regulatory Affairs of the Committee on Government Reform and Oversight of the U.S. House of Representatives.

Regulatory Sunset and Review Act of 1995, H.R. 994, with testimony to the Subcommittee on National Economic Growth, Natural Resources and Regulatory Affirs of the Committee on Government Reform and Oversight of the U.S. House of Representatives.

Lynch v. Household Finance Corp., 405 U.S. 538 (1972)

United State v. Morrison, Vol. 120, Supreme Court Reporter, p. 1740. (2000)

United States v. Lopez, 515 U.S. 55 (1995).

Frothingham v. Mellon, 262 U.S. 447 (1923).

United States v. Butler, 297 US 1. (1936).

Wickard v. Filburn, 317 U.S. 111, 63 S.Ct. 82, 87 L.Ed. 122 (1942)

Index